THINKING VISUALLY

Also available from Continuum

Forsyth: *Career Skills*

Goddard: *Informative Writing*, 2nd Edition

Hamilton: *Passing Exams*

Spencer and Pruss: *Self-Employment*

White: *Dissertation Skills for Business and Management Students*

THINKING VISUALLY

Business applications of fourteen core diagrams

Malcolm Craig Ph.D

continuum
LONDON • NEW YORK

Continuum
The Tower Building
11 York Road
London   SE1 7NX

370 Lexington Avenue
New York
NY   10017-6503

First published 2000
Reprinted 2002
Reprinted 2003

British Library Cataloguing-in-Publication Data
A catalogue record for this book is available from the British Library.

ISBN 0 8264 4833 X

Typeset by Stephen Wright-Bouvier of the Rainwater Consultancy, Faringdon, Oxfordshire.

Printed and bound in Great Britain by Martins the Printers Ltd, Berwick upon Tweed.

Contents

Part 1:   Introduction to diagramming

Part 2:   Applying core diagrams

Part 3:   Introduction to diagramming

Acknowledgements

I thank my wife Margaret for her constant enthusiasm and support, David Barker at Cassell, for initial encouragement and guidance, the staff of the University Library, Cambridge, for their cheerful help, and numerous students on courses of the Open University Systems Faculty. Their work, hopefully enlightening for them, has been enlightening for the author.

I am indebted to the Buzan Organisation for their kind assistance and feedback in the preparation of the Mind Maps® which appear later in this book. Mind Map is a registered trademark of the Buzan Organisation and is used with their enthusiastic permission.

List of figures and tables

Glossary of key terms

Algorithm: A series of steps that follow actions based on yes/no responses to closed questions.

Boundary: A concept that can be represented by objects such as a river, wall, fence or range of hills, but can also be imaginary, to distinguish an area of interest from its environment.

Cause (necessary):   If A is *always* a precursor to any occurrence of B, then A can be said to be a *necessary* cause of B. (B could not be present without A also being present, even though other conditions may be present as well.)

Cause (sufficient):   If action A *always* results in B, then A can be said to be a *sufficient* cause of B. But B could happen without A. (The fact that A always leads to B does not mean that B cannot happen without A.)

Cause (root):   To mean that a number of causes can account for an occurrence, but one fundamental, root, cause can be identified.

Closed-loop control: To mean control of a process where a feed-back loop is in operation, from conditions at the output of a process back to conditions at the input of the process. See Feedback (positive) and (negative).

Effective: To do things appropriately, and to an optimum standard.

Efficient: To do more with less; achieve maximum output from minimum input.

Environment: To mean the area of interest that lies outside a boundary. See *Boundary*.

Feedback (positive):   An action at B that reinforces an earlier behaviour at A that leads, where possible, to a further increase in A's behaviour.

Feedback (negative):   An action at B that corrects behaviour at A to achieve a balance, or homeostasis.

Influence: To mean any influence from A to B such as: power, charisma, economic, positional or wealth. Influence in diagramming terms can be any of these.

Mapping: Essentially to mean the positioning of one thing in a physical, topographical, relation to another. Also has looser meaning of arranging any people, objects and relationship between them.

Relationship: To mean that there is a connection of some kind between A and B.

Preface

This book is an exploration of core diagrams, and how they can be used effectively in business. Fourteen core diagrams have been chosen because together they provide the foundation for a much wider development of diagramming skill. Eventually the range of diagrams anyone can produce is limited only by his or her imagination and inventiveness, but first the fundamental core diagrams should be practised and understood, and this is the main purpose of this book.

In approaching the subject my first idea was to introduce each diagram in turn, in a logical sequence. However, believing that the purpose of diagramming is more important than the diagrams themselves, I have adopted instead a thematic approach. Diagrams do group naturally under themes: for example, some diagrams are more appropriate in managing change, others when thinking about control within a business. A focus of this kind also helps to emphasize the role of diagramming in business situations. Eventually the range of possible diagrams is limited only by imagination. The themes are shown in bold in Figure P.1 as a Relationship diagram. The fourteen core diagrams also appear in this figure, together with some of their variants, and the basic list can be found in the Appendices.

However, although it is extremely helpful to focus on themes in this way when learning to use diagrams, it would be wrong to think of diagrams as being confined to just one theme for ever; when the reader has gained more familiarity with their use, diagrams can be applied in a much more flexible way.

The topics used to illustrate the themes throughout the text have been chosen in the belief that they will all be readily understood by the reader, are relevant to most people, and are sufficiently complex to 'stretch' the use of diagrams. In the case of two of these topics, public transport provision and health care provision, the use of business concepts is relatively new and presents issues ideal for diagramming complexity. In general terms, infrastructure and health are also part of the bedrock of successful business, of whatever kind. Other subjects

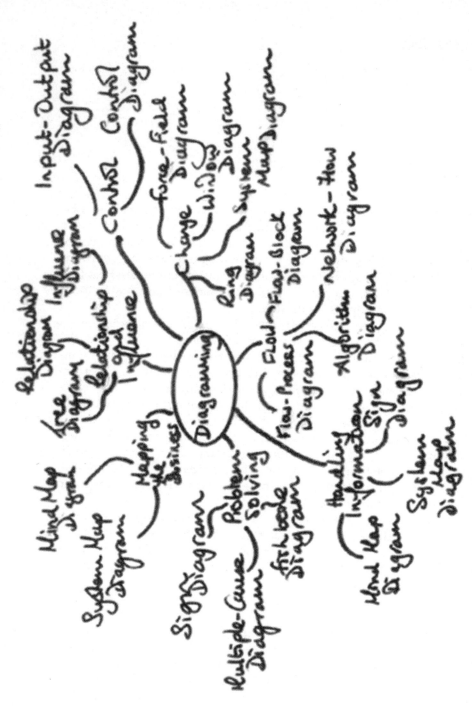

Figure P.1 Relationship diagram of themes in this book

chosen, such as manufacturing and futures trading, cover more traditional business activity.

The book is divided into three parts. Most benefit, and understanding of diagrams, will be gained from reading the three parts in sequence. Alternatively, if you are short of time and need quick access to a 'toolbox' of diagrams, go straight to Part 2, then come back later to Part 1 for a better understanding of the 'basics', and to Part 3 to gain a deeper insight into the theory of the subject. The quick 'toolbox' approach will simply allow you to reproduce diagrams, while a deeper understanding will enable you to develop thorough skill in diagramming.

PART I

Introduction to Diagramming

PART I

1 Personal approaches to diagrams

Handling information

There are many times when it can be helpful to draw a diagram or a picture of some kind, typically when giving directions, explaining an idea or, more ambitiously, helping to solve a complex business problem. Not everyone thinks of diagrams as helpful in these ways: while some people are quick to make a sketch, or a more elaborate graphic creation, others will never do so and often find diagrams quite difficult to follow. Personal differences between people in their approach to diagrams are discussed in the remaining sections of this chapter. 'Diagrammers' will readily reach for any available blank space such as a whiteboard, the back of a document or even a cigarette packet to practise their art. My first experience of someone diagramming on a cigarette packet was when apprenticed in a shipyard. One foreman kept the stub of a pencil behind his ear, ready to make a quick sketch as his way of getting across an idea or instruction. This man handled information by using diagrams along with a whole range of non-verbal signs to help him cope with the very loud noises from drilling and hammering on the ship. Handling information has now become much more problematic; faced with mountains of information, we have to learn how to mine for what we want to know. A diagram in the form of a map, or of relationships between kinds of information, can be enormously helpful in finding our way quickly to the knowledge we need.

Influence of style

After teaching the technique of diagramming to many people, certainly in the hundreds, I have come to recognize a clear difference between those who like to use diagrams and others who would never draw one and who try to avoid their use whenever possible. These represent two extremes, but as in most areas of human behaviour, there is a sizeable group of people who come somewhere in between. Most people being introduced to the use of diagrams go through a transition phase of moving from the familiarity of text to saying the same thing in graphic or pictorial form. It is for this reason that much of this introduction is in text, with only a sprinkling of basic Relationship, Map and Influence Diagrams. Gradually the frequency of diagrams increases as you progress through the book.

Whether you are a keen user of diagrams or someone who avoids them like a plague, it can be helpful to think about the possible reasons that have been put forward for this difference. Research into styles of behaviour can provide us with at least a plausible explanation. Pask and Scott (1972) describe as 'serialist' in their style people who display a preference for handling information in lists, and who like the orderly sequential approach that listing offers. Other people, described as 'holist', prefer to have a general overview, and to work with a more 'pictorial' image.

Figure 1.1, a Relationship diagram, illustrates the main differences in people's approach to diagrams. Overall, in terms of general behaviour, one style does not have any real advantage over the other. But it does appear that people who have a natural preference for listing are more likely to have some difficulty in using diagrams to their full potential. One student, who could be described as an extreme serialist in this respect, began diagramming by making lists; then, to produce a diagram, he drew circles around the lists and joined these with straight lines. Eventually, after much trial and error, the listing was steadily removed and his diagramming technique developed quite well. Lists, like left-to-right text, provide one of the main means of communication, but do have limitations. Lists and text represent a structured orderly approach, while so much in our lives is characterized by complexity or

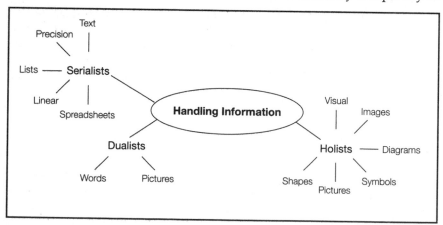

Figure 1.1 Relationship diagram of approaches to handling information

disorder. Think of major issues in business such as lack of skills, inadequate control of finance or resistance to change; you are not likely to find these concisely and easily explained by written text. Diagrams, however, are designed to help us cope with many less orderly or less predictable issues of this kind. Often there are complex, dynamic relationships that become difficult to capture within written text alone.

Left–right brain metaphor

Another way to explain positive or negative attitudes towards diagrams is to use the idea of left- and right-brain difference. People who use images and pictures are often referred to as 'right-brained' in their overall approach. The theory is that the two hemispheres of the brain differ in the way that information is processed. The left side of the brain is said to process information in a way that leads to logical, deductive and linear thinking, while the right side is described as subconscious, intuitive and non-linear in the way it works. The Relationship diagram in Figure 1.2 illustrates how the two halves of the brain can be seen, metaphorically, as handling information in opposite ways, either verbally or visually. Although there is little scientific evidence for such a claim, if valid evidence did exist for a clear visual and non-visual split in brain processing, this could possibly go some way to explaining why certain people take more readily to diagrams and pictures than others.

Where research has been done, however, there is evidence that both sides are capable of handling different types of information. If one side becomes inoperable then the other will adapt so that various functions are maintained. The differences that sparked off this left and right debate are about mental processing times. Quite sophisticated equipment is needed to measure these differences that, in the most significant experiments are rarely above 60 milliseconds. In other words, verbal material when presented to the right visual field (and therefore processed in the left hemisphere) achieves a faster response time than when processed in the right hemisphere. There is no sound justification for transferring these highly specific findings to more general ways of processing information. A psychologist who specializes in handedness, Marian Annett (1985), says that speculation about cerebral specialization quickly outran the facts, so that mythologies of laterality have become established before the evidence could be properly evaluated: 'The most popular accounts of hemisphere specialisation are exaggerated and erroneous.' When people are popularly described as 'right-brained' it is often because they have an artistic, creative or more visual approach to their work. Those described as 'left-brained' are those who deal well with hard data, such as that found in mathematics, and prefer to process information in a sequential way.

To speak metaphorically about right-brained or left-brained thinking

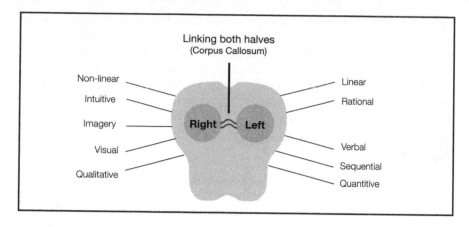

Figure 1.2   Relationship diagram of left–right brain metaphor

can be quite useful when making a point about differences in the way people operate. The metaphor also helps us to think about the development of broader thinking skills, so that we become less reliant on either essentially verbal or visual preferences. To practise diagramming when it is not an automatic preference is one way to develop, in a conscious way, the more visual approach to handling information. Another way is to draw pictures, sometimes called 'rich pictures' as an alternative to the use of text when communicating to others. People who are strongly text-orientated can miss a good deal of insight to be gained from images whether in pictorial or diagrammatic form. The problem is not necessarily the same in the other direction where an emphasis on 'right-brain' thinking could deprive us of more linear and logical thinking. Our approach to education already puts greater emphasis on this 'left-thinking', to use the metaphor. Most teaching, unless delivered by Montessori or Steiner methods, has a strong focus on linear and logical thinking. This early approach is then largely reinforced by the way we behave in business. Various attempts over the years to introduce more creative thinking into business activities can be seen as a means of counteracting our early learning and subsequent emphasis on linear thinking.

Another way of seeing the difference in attitudes to diagramming is to think of doing things logically from first principles, or axioms, as the Greek approach; or being happy to relate one thing to another in a systemic way as the Babylonian approach. Ask yourself: are you a 'Greek' or a 'Babylonian'?

Influence of perception

A diagram reflects a perception of the person who produces it. Where a diagram is the outcome of group or team effort, then it can be assumed to reflect a perception shared by those involved. A definitive diagram, such as the excellent, coloured London Underground map, is rare. When Harry Beck, a 29-year-old engineering draughtsman, illustrated the London tube layout in 1931, he created a diagram that has proved to be remarkably flexible for over 60 years; new stations and new lines have been accommodated quite easily into Beck's diagram. He converted a topographical map (a detailed description of the surface features of a region) into a topological diagram (a diagram showing the geometry of particular chosen features) in a brilliant way. Much later, a bus and tram route diagram, based on Beck's map, was produced for the Amsterdam network by Hans van der Kooi. However, unlike Beck, he could not draw an abstract diagram, since it had to reflect what people saw at street level in Amsterdam if the design was to be readily acceptable. Beck had realized that he could diagram in an abstract way because the system was underground and the public could not see the actual layout. On the tube lines drawn horizontally, stations are farther apart than on vertical lines to allow space for the names. Change of line direction is limited to steps of 45 degrees which can have no relationship to actual layout.

Imagine someone, unaware of the existing London tube diagram, being asked to produce a diagram of the whole underground system on one A4 sheet of paper. The information made available would be a London street map showing the position of tube stations, together with an underground track layout. Even with all available information, it is unlikely that the current masterpiece would be reproduced. Also, if other designers were given, independently, the same task, it is likely that the outcome would be a varied range of diagrams, even though they were working from the same information. The facility that diagramming has to bring out diversity of view between people is a real strength. Different perceptions as well as different ways of approaching the same situation or experience come out through the drawing of diagrams.

The diagram in Figure 1.3 shows one view (perception) of our beliefs being influenced by external events, then our values and beliefs reinforcing each other, with both having a similar relationship to our perceptions. None of these influences (*within the bubble*) are directly observable except through our attitude and behaviour, which again can be seen to reinforce each other. External events influence our behaviour directly, but any reverse influence from behaviour to external influences can be questionable, and may well be drawn as a dotted line. Conventions of this kind in diagramming will be explained in the following chapters.

Drawing diagrams is part of our behaviour and what we produce is the result of a quite complex set of influences. The drawing of a diagram is not simply an image of what we see, like a photographer taking a landscape picture, but is also a reflection of our perceptions, and of all

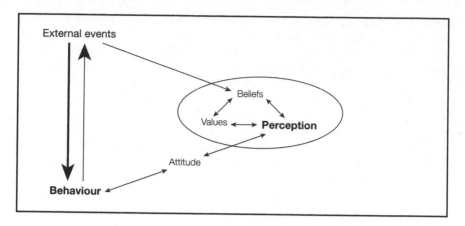

Figure 1.3 Influence diagram of perceptions and behaviour

the influences upon our perceptions. The end result is to have many different ways of representing what we refer to as reality. These differences emerge when people are asked to represent in diagrams what they have witnessed collectively. People in a group seeing exactly the same event are unlikely to have the same information in their diagrams. The photograph, shown here, taken by the famous photo-journalist Alfred Eisenstaedt in 1963, illustrates how at quite a young age we can perceive the same event, in this case a puppet show, very differently. The central figure would have illustrated the event very differently from one of the seemingly frightened children nearby. This picture, which deserves careful examination, can convey more about perception than has been delivered in many hundreds of words on the subject.

Different perceptions of the same problem can lead to difficulties, when they exist in a project team, or a department. In such cases it can be very helpful to draw diagrams of what are seen as the main causes of the problem. The very act of comparing diagrams drawn by various members of the team or department can highlight where such differences exist. Highlighting differences is normally an important first step towards a resolution of the difficulties between members. In such cases the diagrams provide different images reflecting different perspectives, and these can be compared more readily than is possible in open discussion alone.

Although fourteen standard types of diagram, or what we are calling core diagrams, are covered in this book, there are limitless kinds of diagram if we include the variations that can be produced by combining or rearranging these core examples. This book deals only with core diagrams and if you are new to diagramming it is strongly recommended that you follow the conventions given here. When you become more skilled it will be possible to release your creative urge to produce

Figure 1.4   Children at a puppet show

novel pieces of work, but you are strongly advised to learn the fundamental ground-rules first. When you have developed a familiarity with
diagrams it is still worth noting that each diagram you produce should
be able to communicate clearly to others, help enhance their understanding and prompt further thinking on the subject.

Diagrams need to be an integral part of debate. A quite common
practice is to use diagrams only to conclude and summarize what has
been said, and in such cases the real power of diagramming is lost, even
if this method of concluding proves useful at the time. Think of
diagramming as a technique that can be used to start debate and as a
means of generating ideas and ongoing deliberations. Effective diagrams provide us with a language to help us think more clearly, and the
overall aim of this book is to use these various graphical images as tools
for thought.

2 Application of diagrams

Overall purpose of diagramming

Why use diagrams of any kind? This question needs to be answered in a convincing way before many people will be encouraged to put their pencil to a large sheet of paper. First, it is helpful to recognize a general overall purpose behind the use of diagrams. One offering is, 'to unravel and clarify situations in a way that reduces complexity' which is a worthy purpose and one that can be justified when applied to diagramming. We are surrounded by complexity, and some people claim that life is becoming more complex; any tools that can help us simplify situations ought to be very welcome. When, for example, we read about an ongoing troublesome political situation somewhere in the world, whether in the Middle East, Far East or, closer to home, in Ireland, the text is normally full of seemingly contradictory statements. Often there are more than two 'sides' involved in the conflict and the relationships between sides and between the people involved are rarely clear. Similar conflicts occur in business whether within or between departments, or between large organizations. One of the most common actions to resolve such problems is to seek out the facts. But facts have been well described as empty sacks that do not stand up without having contents such as explanation, justification, causes and reason. It is these 'contents' that need to be illustrated in a dynamic way.

Being able to see relationships, whether of influence, cause or control, in a situation that can be disordered, capricious and non-procedural can greatly enhance our understanding of what is going on. As pointed out earlier, so often in our education we are forced along the linear route, and beyond infant classes the pictorial approach to thinking is largely dropped. Although we have been taught to think in a straightjacketing way, in practice we attempt to understand what is going on by forming a kind of mental map in our heads as a means of 'seeing' a picture of events. The basis of this picture is pattern; each person has their own structured pattern, held in the mind, which is not normally available to anyone unless it can be presented in some way. The 'Mind Map' is one way of making this personal picture visible to others. Until this image is down on paper or whiteboard in recorded form, even the person who generates it cannot be sure of the exact contents or relationships that exist between important issues. One term for diagrams of this kind is 'cognitive mapping' – Budwar (1996) and Eden (1990), where the way that someone constructs a picture of what they see as reality can be presented as a diagram. Other people can then 'see' how this person views a particular issue or situation and even the person providing the information to construct the map can learn something about his or her thought processes. However, the overall aim in this book is to use diagrams that can be used as tools to aid our thinking rather than as a means to explore our actual thought processes.

A first drawing in our attempt to unravel a complex situation can be a Relationship diagram based on what has been read and/or heard about the situation. An equally valuable start is to draw a Mind Map, which is a representation of how the person structures and perceives the situation in a quite idiosyncratic way. A Mind Map is unique to the person who produces it, while the Relationship Diagram, similar in appearance, could be produced closely, if not exactly, by another person working on the available information. It is for this reason that giving a title to a diagram is very important. The title should include naming the type of diagram and the subject; notice how diagram titles are written in this book. Think of people going around a modern art exhibition, how they keep bending down to read the titles. Although diagrams are normally far more self-explanatory than such art, a clear title does help set the scene.

Both Relationship and Mind Map can be used at the beginning of many tasks to help illustrate the level of complexity in the situation. Suddenly, while drawing diagrams, you may discover that where a link ought to exist between two components, in practice it cannot be drawn. A missing link of this kind can often be seen as part of the problem or even the problem itself. Further exploration of the diagram can lead to other discoveries, and raises questions about possible causes, leading eventually to explanations. At this point the complex issue is being broken down into smaller manageable parts and boundaries can be drawn around discrete events or problems. Further drawing, using a Multiple-Cause diagram, will begin to clarify what is often a knock-on effect from one causal event to another, and sometimes a breakthrough can be achieved when an ultimate or root cause is located.

Using diagrams to reduce complexity in this way is a skill, and one that has been developed through a literacy programme known as 'Stepping Out'. The programme was first introduced in Australia and is now gaining wider recognition. A range of diagrams is being used to help school pupils understand a piece of text in a way that they can translate into ideas for their own writing. The approach encourages a 'whole' view of literacy to be practised in all school departments as an aid to understanding.

The idea of reducing complexity to a point where clarification becomes possible is given here as an overall purpose in diagramming; from this idea a number of other related purposes emerge. You may find it helpful at this point to check Matrix 1 and Matrix 2, in Appendices A and B, where core diagrams are compared with typical tasks.

Problem-solving

Diagrams can be used extensively in the act of problem-solving. Probably the most important parts of this task are first, problem identification, then clarification and, ultimately, definition. Mistakes made by identifying the wrong problem at an early stage lead almost inevitably to erroneous outcomes later. In business it is possible to take the correct actions and reach the correct solution for the problem as stated, only to find later that the wrong problem has been addressed. When this happens in a chemical plant, for instance, the outcome may amount to thousands of pounds in lost production. A Mind Map, or more than one map from a group of people, will reveal each person's perception of the problem, and the diagram form will often raise questions about the true nature of the problem area, and at times lead to a re-definition of the problem. Sometimes when a key problem has been identified it is discovered from examination of the diagrams that it does not stand alone: there are sub-problems that need to be addressed in order to solve the key problem. A useful approach is to show the various sub-problems in the form of a Tree diagram. Here the problems can be prioritized and various options identified for tackling each one. A diagram of this kind can often lead to serious questions about the validity of the original key problem as stated. Diagrams help us escape from a fixed idea about the problem itself.

It is normal, when presented with a problem, to look as soon as possible for a solution, which in turn leads to a 'tramline' approach to problems. Some problems are solved this way, but too often problems are too complex for this kind of treatment. A well-drawn diagram can show important interactions that too easily can be overlooked. Also, seeing a whole picture in one view is another way to make us question the problem as stated and lead us to what is the true problem. Other core diagrams particularly suited to problem-solving are Multiple-Cause, Fishbone, Force-Field and Control.

Producing ideas

Generally there is no shortage of ideas, so we can think of diagramming as helping to pinpoint potentially good ideas. A diagramming exercise in this context is not like brainstorming or even brain-writing: there is no start point with a blank sheet or a blank mind. There is no forcing of ideas because, instead, we rely upon an idea emerging. Ideas surface largely because diagramming is a systemic process. So many linkages and relationships are on view at a glance that either from the act of drawing or from later observation, the diagram throws up an idea. It is probably true to say that there is more chance of generating a potentially good idea by working with a diagram than by simply waiting, with a drink, for inspiration. When a diagram, completed by one person, is shared among others there is an increased probability of useful ideas being generated. In this case it is often the originator of the diagram who has the idea, or ideas, as a result of listening to others discuss the issue being presented. There needs to be a certain amount of trust here, that the act of diagramming will produce one or more fresh ideas that are likely to be potentially useful. Experience indicates that people seldom come away from a diagramming session totally barren or without at least one useful idea. All core diagrams are capable of prompting ideas; they provide a catalyst that with the right conditions can offer new or changed insights.

Writing reports

Despite certain weaknesses in the use of text, the report is still a vital means of communication. Diagramming and text ought to be seen as complementary, one supporting the other. The use of a diagram during the initial stages of report-writing can be of enormous benefit to the finished product. The format of a report, as recommended in guides to writing, does provide a rationale for the ordering of sub-headings, but not the contents of each section. The subject of the report will often dictate the type of diagram(s) used. A Relationship and/or Influence diagram will help the task of clarifying who and what to include in the report. A Mind Map is useful to highlight the key points as perceived by the writer, and makes it easier to place them in a sequence that best reflects the writer's thinking on the subject. It is useful to write these key points on Post-it notes, place these on a sheet and draw lines of relationship between them. When a pattern has been established, the notes can be put into an order for writing. Such tasks may sound, at first, very time-consuming, but with a little practice such diagramming is done in minutes and normally saves much time in the writing and rewriting of report drafts. An even more important point is that the report ought to read as a well-planned and carefully thought-through document. If the subject of the report is control, then a Control diagram could well be used to clarify the nature and contents of the control being described, even if subsequently the diagram is not used in the report. A Force-Field diagram will help to present both sides of an issue, either as an in-text diagram or as a prompt to the written word. If a report concerns the marketing of a proposed product, then a Window diagram such as SWOT (see Chapter 8) can help ensure that all known strengths, weaknesses, opportunities and threats have been covered within the text. All diagrams presented in this book are suitable as an aid to report-writing; the information gathered from the diagramming simply needs to be relevant to the report contents.

Understanding a process

A good example of a complex process is the automatic feeding of advertising inserts into our daily newspapers. This is done as the newspapers travel on their various tracks between the printing press and the point of stacking ready for delivery by lorry. The electronic control and the exact sequencing of the inserting equipment is difficult to follow by simply observing the process, and any available text is poor at capturing the essence of what is happening. In this case a Flow diagram that breaks down the various operations is a great help in understanding the process. The flow of the different tracks can be drawn, in different colours, on clear transparency material to show the sequence of operations.

The example just given is essentially automatic, but the use of diagramming can be applied equally well to processes where mainly people are involved. It may be necessary to show the flow of money within a business, or the flow of funding into a business or project. A Flow diagram, or a Ring diagram, can be used most effectively when illustrating accounting and finance processes. An Influence diagram can be used to explore the main influences between people working on a flow process, whether in a factory or office. Also, process faults and their causes can be identified and largely diagnosed by using Multiple-Cause and Fishbone diagrams.

Working in groups

Some diagrams such as Control, Tree, Algorithm and Input-Output are better done quietly by an individual or by more than one person working independently. In fact all diagram exercises can benefit from the practice of working independently at the beginning, and then bringing the results together for further work by a group. Where time is critical and a group consensus is needed quickly then other diagrams are better for this task. The diagrams of Relationship, Influence, Multiple-Cause, Fishbone and Window are all particularly suitable for group working from the beginning of a diagram session. The actual choice between these diagrams depends upon the group's task, but the two Matrices in Appendices A and B provide a useful starting point and overall guide. Diagrams can be used too in the exploration of group- or team-working in business. Window, Influence, and Sign diagrams are particularly useful for highlighting how and where groups fail or succeed. For a more comprehensive exploration of why they succeed or fail, refer to Belbin (1981).

Unravelling complex text

Text can be difficult to follow, whether in books, newspapers or furniture assembly instructions. When it is important to understand what is being said in the written word, the diagramming of essential ideas can suddenly bring clarity. When you are able to move issues or ideas around in relationship to each other it becomes easier to see the thread of what has been written. You are simply escaping the left-right and top-down trap that text imposes on our thinking. The Relationship, Influence and Multiple-Cause diagrams are particularly suitable for this task. With some practice, key terms and ideas can be extracted from text and quickly organized into a diagram. This method is especially helpful when essential knowledge needs to be captured in an easily assimilated form, for example during revision for an examination.

Making changes

It is not uncommon to read and hear a statement from the media that nobody likes change. Only one person who likes change needs to be found to disprove this statement, and I myself have come across many people who simply love change and normally cannot get enough of it. One of the few certainties is that things must change – nature tells us this all the time. The issue is not so much whether to change, but how to change in the most effective way. If we can accept that life has no certainty, then it is possible to enjoy the experience of change. The main role of diagramming here is to handle changing situations more effectively and efficiently. The Force-Field diagram helps us to confront the all too common for-and-against reactions of people confronted with change. The window diagram encourages us to see things in different ways and helps us to see how changes can be made. The Input-Output and Control diagrams do this too, using a rather more structured approach. Other diagrams to encourage balanced thinking about change in this way are Map, Multiple-Cause, Ring and Sign.

In the words of change-management there is an unfreezing of the existing state, and eventually a re-freezing into the new state after the change has been made. On both occasions it is possible to use diagrams to compare differences between the before-change state and the after-change state. The System Map diagram and Influence diagram are especially suitable for making this comparison. Even before the change takes place a diagram can be developed for the current state, and another diagram that anticipates the new state. The images produced can be of great benefit during the planning stages. This method of comparing before and after diagrams is discussed again in the influence section.

Mining for knowledge

Information overload is a commonly heard term in business, but there can be some confusion between information and knowledge. Information provides one source of knowledge; other sources are observation, experience and feelings. Information is often imposed on us from outside and little control exists to help us stem the flow. In contrast, knowledge is what we extract from many sources; it is the state of knowing. Knowledge, unlike information, is, or ought to be, well within our control. The first step in being more efficient in the handling of knowledge is to manage information. If we use the metaphor of an information mountain, then we need to know where and how to mine for essential knowledge. Using a System Map, it is possible to draw a boundary around what needs to be known, the knowledge system, and identify the sources of information outside the boundary. This map begins to lay out the territory and allows us to remove extraneous sources of information that impose themselves without offering anything in return. Sometimes a source of information becomes so crucial to the business that it is drawn inside the boundary. Knowing where to go quickly for knowledge, and how to filter out extraneous information, is becoming an essential skill in business. The Control diagram can also be used to demonstrate how information is controlled within a business. Similarly the Influence diagram helps us identify the important influences upon information management and mining for knowledge.

Summary

In summarizing the purpose of diagramming, it can be said that all core diagrams, and their various offshoots, can help us think about issues around us. Instead of walking about for days, months or even years with niggling problems, or a good idea, being tossed around in the head, it is worth giving air to these thoughts by producing diagrams. It is from these 'pictures' that solutions and pointers to the way forward can emerge. The main purpose of diagramming is to help simplify everyday tasks such as:

- problem solving;
- writing reports;
- making changes; and
- coping with information overload.

3 Drawing, reading and interpreting diagrams

Tools for diagramming

The basic tools, and probably the most effective in helping us to think with diagrams, are a soft B pencil, a sharpener, an eraser, coloured pens or pencils, and preferably a blank A3-size sheet of paper. Although working areas the size of a cigarette packet are still used, such cramping can hinder expansiveness of ideas. Producing a diagram on a small piece of paper, even of A5 or A4 size, does seem to cramp thinking; a reasonable-sized 'canvas' helps create boldness and a wider range of ideas. Another advantage of the bigger area is that some otherwise discarded work can remain to show how your thinking has been developing towards the final diagram. With these basic tools you can draw in any location: office, building site, sales floor or at home. The diagram can be modified as ideas come to mind and friends or colleagues may gather around to help spark off ideas as you draw. If those who have been involved in the drawing walk away to do something else, or simply allow time to ponder, the time away can often help produce other ideas when they return.

A white- or blackboard, apart from a lack of portability, will serve the same purpose as a large sheet of paper equally well. A major advantage of the whiteboard is that a small group can more easily gather around and either work through the person drawing the diagram or become fully involved themselves by taking control of the pen. It is important with whiteboards to use the right pen. If in doubt try a small trial mark to check that it can be removed easily. If it is the wrong pen, and as usual no cleaning spirit is handy, over-writing with a correct, non-permanent, pen will remove the stubborn mark.

Another valuable aid to the use of diagrams is the overhead projector (OHP). With this equipment it is possible to overlay two or more transparencies and build up a complete diagram. Non-permanent transparency pens need to be used so that changes can be made to the diagram as the discussion develops and new ideas come to mind. This method is especially useful when you have to think through a really complex issue or to understand an involved manufacturing process. Take, for instance, the example of the typical oil refinery with many pipes linked in a maze-like formation. Following or learning to understand what goes where is quite difficult from observation or from any written text. If the different levels of flow are separated out and diagrammed, in colours, on individual transparencies it is much easier to build up a picture of what is happening by overlaying transparencies on the overhead projector. Diagrams produced and held on a personal computer can also be presented through a plate positioned on an overhead projector, not as in a formal presentation but as an active diagramming session where Diagrams can be changed in response to ideas. The development of visual-aid equipment allows for direct viewing of diagrams held on laptop computers. By using diagramming software, available through the Internet, it is possible to manipulate diagrams held on a laptop or desktop computer. The key words 'diagramming' or 'diagrammer' will locate necessary software through the common search engines. Referencing of this material here is unreliable because products and providers change so rapidly, and information becomes quickly out of date.

The drawing of diagrams as permanent 'masterpieces' should normally be avoided; the diagrams described here are tools for thought, and when thinking has been done the diagrams can often go into a waste bin. The hand drawing can be quite rough in outline provided it communicates an idea. The bubbles, boxes and arrows in a diagram can be done quickly to illustrate a process or to give direction. The same is true of pictures where stick people and symbols are used to illustrate an issue and possible solution. See, for example, Figure 3.1.

Such illustrations, often known as 'rich pictures', can often uncover aspects of a problem where discussion or written text have failed. The images can be drawn with equal effectiveness whether by hand or using software, as in Figure 3.1 with Microsoft PowerPoint. A further example using images in this way is given in Chapter 8. During my work with Open University students, one blind student in a group developed a rich picture with Braille and used the principle of the Multiple Cause diagram by arranging formula in a spreadsheet to show, in a matrix way, that (for example) the component in A2 was a causing component in F3, and the component in B4 was also a cause of F3. Conventional diagramming was done by having someone draw to his instructions. Other students in the group could then debate his diagram, and a good deal was learned about diagrams and their uses in this way.

An exception to the quick sketch that solves a problem and then goes into the waste bin, is when a particular diagram can be formally printed in a document, so that it passes from being a tool for thought to become a more permanent record. But even when used as a permanent record

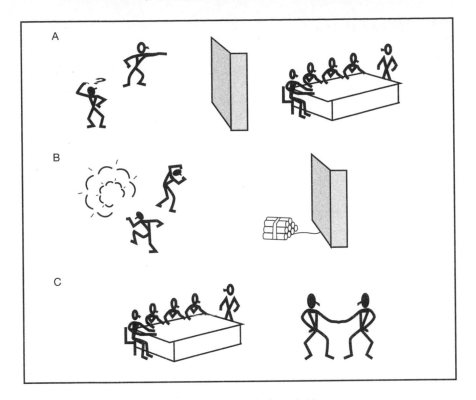

Figure 3.1   Use of pictorial image

the diagram will have performed its main purpose before being seen on the printed page. A perfectly effective and useful diagram could be produced on a beach by drawing in the sand with a stick, even when the tide is coming in. For those who are reluctant to draw images, or say 'Oh I cannot draw,' a very good guide is provided by Betty Edwards (1982), in a book about drawing from the right side of the brain.

Computer graphics provide another very useful medium for diagramming, and by networking computers it is possible for a number of people to share in the development of a diagram as part of an ongoing discussion. The development of a diagram and sharing of the necessary thinking can be done very well at remote locations by using this kind of networking. Most monitor screens are not of the preferred A3 size but this, apart from a natural aversion of some people to computers, is possibly the only limitation.

The overall message is to draw in a way that suits you; the observations above are simply those that have made sense to me when using graphical aids to thinking over a number of years. For people who prefer lists or text, the best start into diagramming is to generate a list of main points, and then from this list begin developing a diagram.

Building blocks

The basic building blocks of diagrams could consist of any shape or symbol we are capable of drawing. The same could be said of writing – just reflect on the differences between Chinese, Arabic and English text. Although very different, each language adopts conventions in shaping the words so that people who understand the language can communicate through a shared understanding of these conventions. The same is true of diagramming; there are conventions that can be shared among people who communicate and help their thinking through diagrams. The accepted shapes and symbols of diagrams can be rearranged in numerous different ways, just as words are rearranged in what we know as writing style. Table 3.1 shows the various diagram building blocks with the respective functions they serve.

Drawing straight solid lines on a diagram is a simple enough task but to communicate clearly we need to think about how the lines are to be drawn. A straight line is used to indicate a relationship of some kind between a person A and another person B, or between tasks, events or objects. There is no arrow to indicate direction – the line shows only that a relationship exists. The actual kind of relationship comes from 'reading' the diagram by asking 'What is this telling me?'

There are times when we have insufficient information about a possible relationship between an A and a B, and here it is better to use a broken straight line, to be either removed or filled in as solid later, when knowledge has been gained.

Arrows show essentially direction; flow, influence and causation are directional. Flow and influence can be two-way between an A and a B; sometimes the flow or influence is equal in each direction and a double-headed arrow can be used. Where influences or flow are unequal we draw a thick arrow one way and a thinner arrow in the reverse direction. Causation is always unidirectional: it cannot be reversed. If B is caused by A, then the arrow can only go from A to B. Reflect on the chicken and egg dilemma.

The shapes of square and rectangle are interchangeable and these 'boxes' hold information that is essentially objective, clear and unambiguous; the 'squareness' is symbolic of hard-type information that is predictable and reasonably certain. When we draw irregular shapes or 'bubbles' the implication is that information is of the soft type where a degree of doubt, ambiguity and uncertainty normally exists. When Voltaire said, 'Doubt is uncomfortable, certainty is ridiculous,' he was close to the truth, but we put in boxes what we perceive to be more certain than the contents of bubbles. The outcome is that boxes tend to be used in diagrams of manufacturing, financial movement, control,

LINES AND SHAPES	FUNCTION
STRAIGHT SOLID LINE	linear, sequential, direct relationship between A and B
CURVED SOLID LINE	circular process of relationship leading back to source
BROKEN LINE	uncertainty or questioning of relationship
SINGLE-HEADED ARROW	shows direction of flow, influence or causation
DOUBLE-HEADED ARROW	shows equal two-way interaction between an A and a B
THICK ARROW ONE WAY, THINNER ARROW THE OTHER WAY	shows unequal two-way influences between A and B
SQUARE OR RECTANGLE	carries objective, measurable, unambiguous statements
IRREGULAR SHAPE (BUBBLE)	carries subjective statements and 'people' involvement
CIRCLE	starting and end points of a process or algorithm
CROSS WITHIN A CIRCLE	a comparator in a control process (Control diagram)
DIAMOND	making decisions normally of Yes/No type

SYMBOLS	
LIGHT BULB	shows that Idea(s) exist(s)
CROSSED SWORDS	shows conflict
TANGLED ROPE	shows complexity
BRICK WALL	shows an obstacle
SKULL AND CROSSBONES	shows danger
ONE-TON WEIGHT	shows pressure
LINKED HANDS	shows harmony
QUESTION MARK	shows questioning
KNOTTED ROPE	shows that a problem exists
EXCLAMATION MARK IN CIRCLE	shows a solution
DIAGONAL LINE IN CIRCLE	shows a practice not allowed

Table 3.1 Diagram building blocks

project-planning and networking. Bubbles, in contrast, appear wherever there is either strong or exclusively human involvement.

Drawing lines and shapes in different ways adds greatly to the power of a diagram, especially when many are used together in one diagram. The symbols listed in Table 3.1 are, or should be, self-explanatory and add further to the richness of communicating and thinking with diagrams.

Reading diagrams

If you prefer to read information in lists, it is likely that diagrams appear at first sight a rather disjointed ambiguous muddle, while other people scan a diagram and seem to read it like the written page. The place to begin in reading any diagram is the title. A well formed title will show the type of diagram, and the key subject. As an example here are some titles taken from the pages of this book:

- Systems Map of a GP's practice
- Control diagram of futures processing
- Multiple-Cause diagram of declining demand for public transport
- Fishbone diagram of failure to meet project deadlines.

Diagrams ought to be linked directly, through the title, to a specific event, failure, opportunity or problem. The scene has been set and you can begin to read the diagram itself in context.

The next step is to look for a 'beginning' and an 'end point' in the diagram – is it possible to read from start to finish? If this is the case then it is likely that there will be arrows to show direction from one end to the other. Failure of a project, or of an aircraft, is likely to have a diagram of this pattern. A diagram of a manufacturing process, or a project plan, would be even more likely to have this pattern. If there is no obvious start or finish you will be reading about relationship or influence, with much interaction, and quite possibly complexity. Influences on motivation at work or on lack of profitability are likely to produce a diagram where start and finish are difficult or impossible to locate. A third possibility is that the start can also be the finish, as in Ring diagrams, which show an ongoing circular process. A diagram showing the management of change will have this circular pattern because the final outcome and lessons learned from one change feed into the beginning of the next change, or should do.

By now you ought to have a feel for the kind of diagram, whether it is linear, logical and flow-like, or whether it is more complex with many different interactions that make it difficult to get a clear focus. In these circumstances a well drawn diagram should simply be reflecting reality.

The title of a diagram ought to state Relationship, Influence, Force, Flow, Multiple-cause or Map, so that the lines or arrows on the diagram are read in this way. Lines, *not arrows,* on a Relationship diagram are read as indicating some kind of relationship between an A and a B. An arrow on an Influence diagram reads as: A has an influence on B; and a second arrow indicates that B also has an influence on A. Different thickness of arrow shows relative estimated strength of influence. Each arrow, *not just a line,* on a Multiple-Cause diagram is read as: A is the cause of B (deeper reading can be done around necessary and sufficient cause – see Chapter 7). There are *no* lines (with or without arrows) joining components on a System Map, because it serves the true purpose of a map to indicate location and not relationship, influence, flow or cause of any kind.

Other diagrams loosely called Maps, such as Cognitive Maps and Mind Maps do have lines, but the meaning of the lines is not clear from the title. In the case of Cognitive Maps, as pointed out earlier (p. 12), you need to know about George Kelly's construct theory (1955) to understand these diagrams fully, and to avoid misuse of the diagram.

Where the title refers to a Flow diagram, each arrow represents movement: the flow of activities in project planning such as are found in a Flow-Process diagram, or when making decisions as in an Algorithm diagram. Other kinds of flow are to be found in passing from one manufacturing stage to the next, where assemblies or components flow along a production line.

Lines can also have different meaning within the same diagram. The Control diagram provides a good example of this (Chapter 6). There are lines showing inputs into the process being controlled; and also lines to show outputs and feedback. Where lines have different meanings in a diagram it is important to label them. In a Multiple-Cause diagram all single-headed lines can be taken to be causal; in the Control diagram you need to label all lines. Labelled lines are read in the same way as unlabelled. The feedback line on a Control diagram needs to be read as feedback through word of mouth, electronically or by pro-forma. Similarly the line from the Comparator to Activators in a Control diagram represents an action of some kind and how this actually happens needs to be understood. A practised map-reader, walking the hills, does not 'see' contour lines on his map but reads these as a slope of a certain steepness. If there is also shaded hachuring, it is crags that he or she sees. The skilled diagrammer reads the symbols and lines of a diagram in a similar way; a feedback line is seen as the method used to facilitate this feedback.

This description of reading diagrams appears to be rather fragmented because it has been necessary to isolate the building blocks in order to explain how they are read. With practice, the reading of lines, shapes and symbols comes together in one whole. In surprisingly little time you can scan a diagram and read the contents as though they were physically spread out before you.

Interpreting diagrams

When interpreting a diagram you begin by asking a basic question referred to already: 'What is this diagram telling me?' Even when the diagram has been drawn by yourself it greatly helps thinking to step back, have a cup of coffee, and return to ask this question.

An Influence diagram from Chapter 5 is reproduced here in Figure 3.2 so that it can be 'talked through' and interpreted. The title tells us that each line represents perceived influence within a GP's practice. Practices of this kind are increasingly being managed as businesses. The practice itself is contained within the main bubble. There are many uncertainties, human behaviours and poor predictability, so a bubble is quite appropriate. There is an arrow showing uncertainty in this practice between access to health records and patients' needs. Before the early 1990s there would have been no arrows of influence here; there was no access for patients, so influence of any kind was not possible. Since the introduction of computerized records and data protection legislation some influence is now possible, but still the actual situation is unclear with respect to manual records. If this diagram had been produced over five years ago, this anomaly would be clear. Interpreting influences within a boundary normally leads to the observation that all components within the boundary influence each other. Where a gap exists, as between records and patients, warning bells ought to be ringing that something is missing. This diagram shows changing practices: funding policy and waiting lists are relatively new, and further interpretation can reveal how there is a knock-on effect to the influence between GPs and patients. The changes being made to activities within the boundary lead to an increase in the managing function so as to cope with increased influences from both within and outside the boundary. The overall picture is complex; the GP is influenced directly and indirectly from many sources going back eventually to the Health Minister. The implication is that such influences must be very difficult to manage well.

Part of interpreting a diagram is to ask what may be missing. You may well have picked up on missing items from this diagram. One major example is the influence that makers and suppliers of pharmaceutical products have upon this business. Another is the location of the practice; whether the environment is rural or industrial makes a significant difference to the amount and kinds of influence upon the practice.

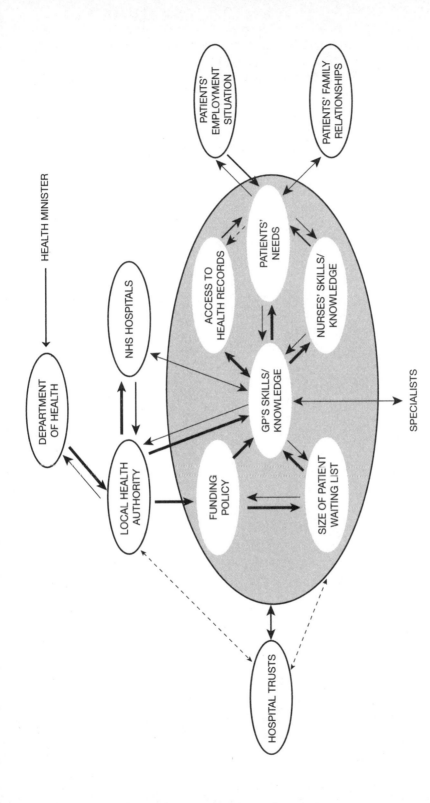

Figure 3.2 Copy of influence diagram of a GP's practice

When the diagram is challenged in this way it can be said to be serving a useful purpose. The debate is widened, a more complete picture begins to emerge and clearer understanding of any problems becomes possible.

PART II

Applying the Core Diagrams

4   Mapping the business

The Map

An Ordnance Survey map represents what we can expect to find on the ground. It is a representation, rather than an absolutely faithful copy, of what exists. However, in practice the map can provide vivid pictures when in the hands of a skilled reader. Instead of seeing only a maze of contour lines on the map, the image seen in the mind of the reader can be of a deep narrow valley, a wide open moor, or steep cliffs. The late Alfred Wainwright, writer of detailed and creative English Lakeland guide-books, once said he much preferred a map to a book, and this ability to 'read into' diagrams is an advanced stage of the diagrammer's art. All diagrams need to be 'read' in this way, to provide a picture or a story.

There are two kinds of map: one is physical or as close as we can get to reality by diagramming, and the other is mental (sometimes referred to as cognitive), a map of what we perceive reality to be. Maps that reflect the physical are used to describe a wide range of subjects such as land form, the sky, geology, or even an organization. Maps that reflect our mental processes are known as Mind Maps and Cognitive Maps. Mind Maps are explored as an example of a core diagram because they have a direct relevance to business processes. Cognitive Maps in contrast are more concerned with how different people demonstrate a 'map' of reality as they see it in their minds; even though business has extended the use beyond a purely cognitive area, it is in understanding mental constructs that the strength of the Cognitive Map lies.

A further kind of mental mapping is provided by the System map. This allows for the representation of people and events in groups or, in organizations, more widely.

The System Map

One diagram related to the activity of people, rather than of land mass, is called a System Map. A System Map of a company or a department can be very useful; in effect it shows the geography of the place. A first useful exercise is to draw a basic diagram in the form of a System Map. Like an Ordnance Survey map this diagram does not show influence, cause, flow or control of any kind. As in the conventional map, only relative position is shown or the spatial relationship of one thing to another. The General Practitioners' (GPs') practice (business) is shown in Figure 4.1. It has been chosen because most readers will have views and ideas about how a business of this kind functions.

The significant features to be noted when reading a System Map are:

* boundary
* environment
* elements
* sub-systems.

The last two of these four are generally referred to as components. The *boundary* separates the central components from components outside, in the environment. 'Boundary' in this sense is conceptual and not necessarily real and physical like a wall or a river. A boundary is often visualized as being a reasonable divide between those things that are an integral part of what we see as the system, in this case a GPs' practice, and everything else that is related, but outside the system, or outside the boundary. We conceptualize the boundary in this way, and see it personally as we wish. The Berlin wall was just that, a wall, yet some people chose to conceptualize it as a barrier, while others conceptualized it as a boundary: two quite different views of the same thing. Boundaries, like barriers, only really exist in the mind; in reality we are looking at walls, fences, or obstacles of some kind that may or may not be physical. A manager could make a policy change that could be described as creating a barrier to further progress, or members of a department may put a boundary around themselves by not communicating with others, the wall in Figure 3.1 being an example. The boundary drawn on a Systems Map is conceptual in this way. The GPs' System Map shows a boundary as conceptualized by a user of the system; a GP could well draw its position differently.

The *system environment* is always there; without it, what we see as the system would be totally isolated inside the boundary. Also, without an environment there would be little point in having a boundary. The view of Buddhist monks as being totally self-sufficient inside a Himalayan monastery might come nearest to a closed system. Otherwise, most areas of human activity have what can be called an environment that is peculiar to their various activities. The term often used is 'an open system', and in practice some systems are more open than others,

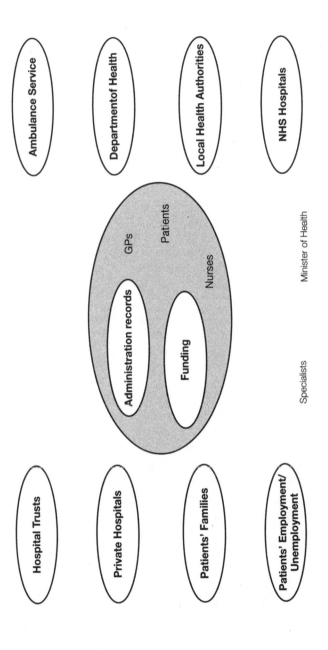

Figure 4.1 System map of a GP's practice

but all can be described as 'open'. Again, different people within the same boundary may view the composition of their environment differently. If each person working in a GPs' practice was asked to produce a System Map by seeing their department as a system in this way, a number of differences would be observed, because again their various perceptions would influence how they see the practice and its environment. The main point about the environment is that it does not embrace the whole universe out there: only the people and things operationally related in some way to events inside the boundary are included as 'environment'. The environment can be said to consist of people, things and events said to influence certain people, things and events inside the boundary. Influence acts in the other direction too, from within the boundary to the environment. But remember, the System Map like all maps can show only relative position of one thing and another; it does not show influence, control, flow or cause of any kind. For these we must turn to other diagrams.

The *elements* are people or things that we are not wishing to reduce further; they stand alone. Typically a person, or one specific activity, can be seen as an element. In the GPs' map above, individual people such as GPs, patients, nurses and specialists are seen not as sub-systems but as elements.

The *sub-system* in contrast will be seen as containing a number of elements and can be broken down into smaller parts. In the GPs' System Map a number of elements can be included in the administration sub-system. In addition to health records there are clerks, computers and schedules.

The whole map is made up of sub-systems and the sub-systems are made up of elements, not unlike a set of Russian dolls. To use a practical example, think of a road planner's view of the motor car. To this person, the vehicle is seen as an element in the planning because there is no point in reducing it further. However, to a motor mechanic the vehicle can be seen as a complete system that consists of various sub-systems such as braking, ignition, fuel and suspension. Each of these sub-systems consists of elements that the mechanic is not likely to break down further, but will simply replace, for example, the spark plugs within the ignition sub-system. In the case of diagrams both elements and sub-systems are commonly referred to collectively as 'components'. Returning to the System Map diagram of the GPs' practice, we can see that some components are shown as elements because I perceive them as individuals standing alone. Other components, such as Funding and Local Health Authority, are shown as sub-systems. A number of elements and activities can be contained within these sub-boundaries and it may be necessary to break down any one of these sub-systems at some time, as a means of clarifying some of the complexity.

BUSINESS APPLICATION OF SYSTEM MAPS

Sometimes a System Map and some other diagrams are drawn with overlapping bubbles. In Figure 4.2 the example given by (a) and (b) is questionable practice because logically it is never clear what the relationship is at the overlapped area or between the components in the respective bubbles. This diagramming arrangement is better known as the diagrams developed by John Venn in the late nineteenth century. The subject is covered fully in more specialized logic diagrams. See Allwein (1996) and Shin (1994). In business application it is generally more helpful to show such overlapping relationship as either a Relationship diagram or an Influence diagram, depending upon the depth of interaction.

A more realistic demonstration of an overlapping bubbles diagram is given by (c). The three primary additive colours of green, red and blue in equal proportions give white light, and various mixes give yellow, cyan and magenta. This is a more appropriate use of bubbles in a diagram.

A System Map, which you should note from Figures 4.1 and 4.3 has no overlapping bubbles, is a snapshot in time, a frozen image that reflects only what is observed at that moment. Even as I write, the map of the GPs' practice is about to change significantly. The major change is to the funding sub-system, which in turn may change other positions on the map. It is not unlike deciding to build a dam or divert a river and waiting to see what changes need to be made to the existing map. There

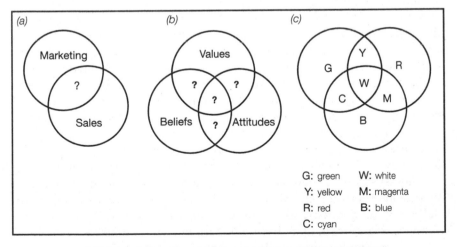

Figure 4.2 Overlapping bubbles (Venn diagram)

is much information we still need to know about the 'picture' being provided by this map. What influence does the Health Minister have over this system? What is the relationship with trust hospitals? These questions and more can be addressed by using other diagrams. Like all maps, this one is very good as a means of orientating ourselves to the many features of the subject. As pointed out earlier, it is the 'geography' of a company or a department. The General Practitioners (GPs) who some years ago could be said to have almost total control over events within the practice, now find themselves facing additional influences that are difficult to control, from outside the boundary. They need to add skills of business management to those of medicine, but also they need to know what has to be managed, both within and outside the boundary. The map is an excellent way to set out the territory.

Another example of the System Map in use concerns the problematic area of public transport provision. In this case the map helps to reduce much of the complexity to manageable chunks, that can be treated as separate but related issues.

In some countries, transport is a national integrated resource that comes within a national boundary, while in other countries the resource is divided among many businesses. The boundary shown in Figure 4.3 is critical in showing a clear difference between the central components of a public transport company and the many influences that exist within this system's environment. As pointed out earlier, this map can only be a snapshot in time, and it is here that a major dilemma exists. Most people like to have a clear picture of where they are and what is going on, and a map can be a very useful tool for satisfying this need. Unfortunately, maps portraying issues or organizations are rarely constant. Looking at the public transport map, the transport integration sub-system can disappear quite quickly; maintenance could be sub-contracted out and cease to be seen as part of provision, there is the dilemma that public need is now satisfied by mainly private provision, and so on. However, the map can give us a reference point in trying to understand what is happening; without this we could effectively be lost.

We can choose to see any area of human activity in this way and the drawing of a System Map helps us to illustrate the current position of elements, sub-systems, boundaries and the contents of the chosen system's environment. We could take any component in Figure 4.3, such as transport policy or vehicle maintenance, and regard it as a system in its own right. The vehicle maintenance System Map would show different sub-systems, elements, boundary and environment relevant to vehicle maintenance. It is this diagram that should be considered in any deliberations about plans to contract out this service. Before making changes to any form of activity it is wise to draw a map of this kind. If any sub-system is removed, then the whole system will be influenced in

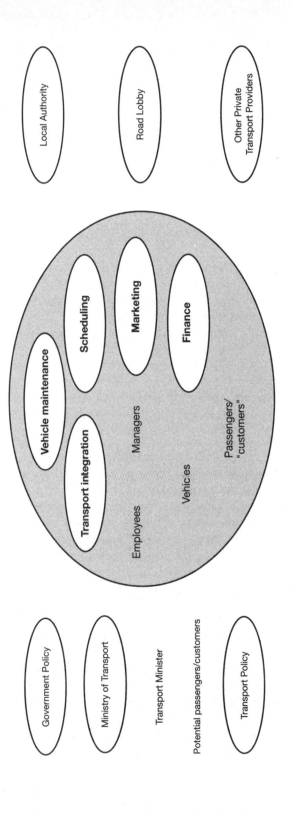

Figure 4.3 System map of a public transport company

some way. This 'whole' effect can often be ignored when changes of this kind are proposed, and a new diagram, reflecting the proposed change, helps us to understand possible consequences of the change.

BUSINESS PURPOSES OF THE SYSTEM MAP

Drawing a System Map of a company or a department known to you should provide the opportunity to generate some key questions: If important business questions are not viable, the answers are unlikely to be viable.

- Who, within the boundary, has real control over components within the environment?
- What are the implications for people within the boundary if control over the environment is poor or non-existent?
- What would happen to the company or department if any one component was removed from within the boundary?
- Who within the boundary has regular and meaningful contact with components outside the boundary?
- What changes could be made to the map that would promise improvement?
- How far can the activities within the boundary be rationalized, while still maintaining the viability of the business?

More questions can be raised, depending upon the subject chosen for mapping. Issues can emerge from a map through the very act of diagramming. It can also be useful to draw one map before making a planned change, and a second map showing the planned position of components after the change. A before-and-after comparison can raise issues that could otherwise be overlooked. Using maps to facilitate change allows a more complete 'whole' picture to be seen.

SUMMARY AND CONVENTIONS

In business, the term 'map' is used very loosely indeed – almost any configuration of words, boxes or bubbles can be passed off as having 'mapped a process'. Strictly speaking a map is designed to show the relative position of things to each other, and any diagram that does this, and only this, can suitably be described as a map. The System Map and Mind Map both fulfil this basic aim, even though their different format leads to different uses and interpretations. Confusion can occur when drawers or readers of this type of diagram attempt to convey more than is possible with it. It is not possible to look at a Map diagram and automatically extract from it causation or influence, as you can with a Multiple-Cause diagram or Influence diagram respectively.

Conventions for the system map

- It shows only position of components relative to each other.
- No lines of influence, relationship or cause are to be included.
- The system boundary is conceptual rather than physical.
- The way sub-systems and elements are shown depends upon how the diagrammer perceives these components.
- It is a snapshot in time and not predictive of what may happen in the future.

The Mind Map

The Mind Map has been developed by Tony Buzan, and 'Mind Map' is a recognized trade mark of the Buzan Organization. The most complete guide is provided by *The Mind Map Book*, published by BBC Books in 1993. There is also *MindManager* software available from Buzan Centres. Some initial ideas were inspired by the early work of Michael Howe (1970). Howe studied note-taking practices of students, and one important finding was that students who recorded no more than three key words in a sentence could recall the subject as well as students who had tried to record the entire text. Howe also developed an efficiency ratio for note taking by dividing the number of ideas successfully recorded by the number of words needed to record them. From this a significant positive correlation was found between the most efficient note-takers and subsequent recall rate of the students. This could simply mean that students who are better at recall also have more efficient note-taking skills. However, despite this reservation, the important role of key words in helping recall was established. Mind Maps are based upon the efficient use of key words linked together in such a way that they represent the diagrammer's way of thinking about the subject.

There can be as many ways to construct reality in our heads as there are people. As pointed out earlier, the Mind Map is a diagram unique to the drawer.

BUSINESS APPLICATIONS OF THE MIND MAP

The Mind Map in Figure 4.4 is a snapshot of the factors seen as relevant to public transport provision at one particular time.

The central bubble provides a focus: the main subject being mapped. Other bubbles show key words associated with the subject, that is, 'key'

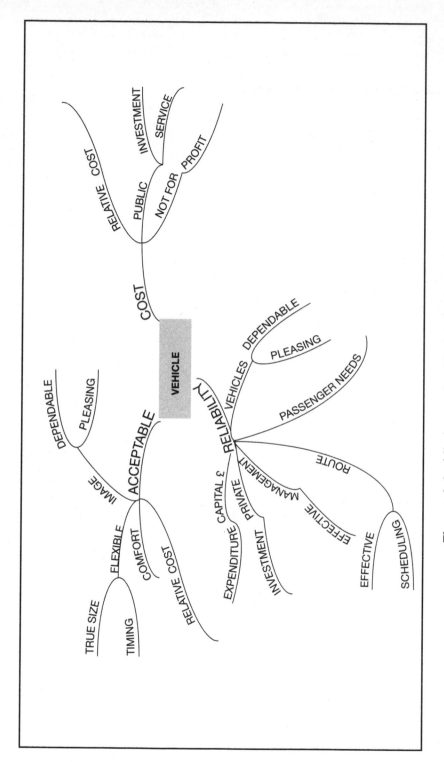

Figure 4.4 Mind map of public transport provision

in the mind of the drawer. From these key words other important features emerge in a web-like way. The diagram format shown here is the 'core' approach; in time you will develop your own preferred way to cluster key words and important features around the central subject. The impact of the diagram can be enhanced by the use of different colours for each set of constructs, by coloured arrows, symbols or pictures.

This diagram is not taken from any available printed information, but is simply the way one person who has the perspective of a user mentally constructs the subject of public transport provision. The very act of drawing this diagram generates a number of ideas about the subject: the 'trigger' words such as 'cost' or 'reliability' help us to see an overall picture because they in turn trigger further images, and the connecting links come to mind as one draws rather than being fitted in at the end. Anyone 'reading' this diagram should realize that cost, reliability and acceptability are not compartmentalized like this. There must be lines that can be drawn between the three sets of components. The lines can be of relationship or of influence, so a new drawing could be done to include all these components as part of a Relationship diagram or an Influence diagram, or better still, one of each. Unlike other diagrams, the Mind Map does not have to indicate relationship, influence, control, force or cause. The links in a Mind Map can be of any connection that anyone can possibly think of. As I said earlier, this diagram provides an idiosyncratic image.

For a person writing a report on the subject of public transport provision this diagram would serve as a very useful starting point. The exercise would help highlight key features and provide a possible order for sections in the report.

One potential problem when using Mind Maps to plan written work is that the contents can present a view too personal for 'official' consumption. The outcome can too easily become a controversial document. The preferred approach is to consult others to check sensitive areas within the map and if possible make use of Mind Maps done by colleagues.

The next Mind Map (Figure 4.5) shows features of planning budgets in a manufacturing business. Managers in different manufacturing companies may well have different views when planning budgets; the important point is that a diagram of this kind can spark debate about the true relationships between budgets, and what actually drives the establishment of budget control.

Mind Maps can be drawn about anything – yes, anything! Subjects to go into the central bubble could be: personal finance, company finance, marketing strategy, project failure, holiday location or moving home.

Mind Maps are very useful aids to assist memory. Some people, as pointed out in the introduction, are happier to memorize information in

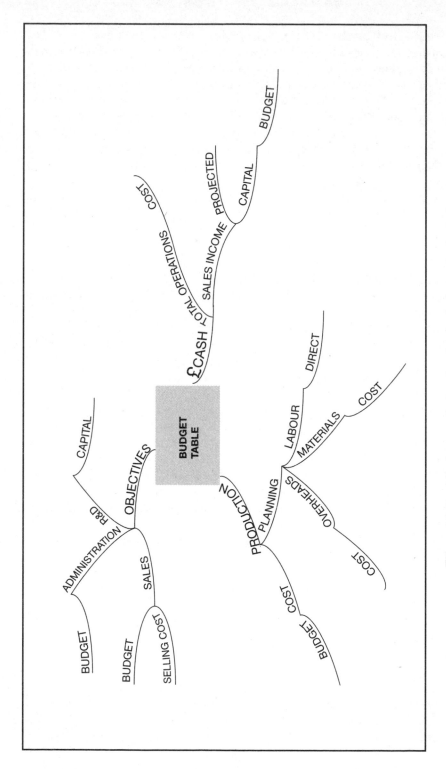

Figure 4.5 Mind map of planning budgets for manufacturing

lists, but from what we understand about memory it is preferable to recognize associations between different blocks of information. Memory is not unlike a filing cabinet: a particular key is needed to open up a file of information. When you cannot remember a name, for example, a helpful idea is mentally to run through the alphabet. You can often narrow the possibility of the first letter of the name to no more than two or three letters, and then suddenly the one correct first letter triggers access to the name. The first letter has taken you to the right place in your mental filing cabinet. The difficulty some people have is in remembering the vital key word. When a Mind Map has been drawn to reflect your own unique way of ordering information, with key words that are unique to you there is a much improved chance of recalling the needed information. Generally it is easier to see the image of a picture, which is what a diagram is, than to 'see' information in text form. When drawing the Mind Map, the future recall is greatly helped by printing key words in capitals, and by using colour.

In meetings or lectures the Mind Map allows you to spend more time listening, the most important skill in these circumstances, and less time in writing. Key words and phrases with linking lines are all that is needed; any further detail can be added soon afterwards. The skill of mind-mapping in this context does need some practice, but gradually the level of efficiency in note-taking can improve beyond recognition.

When looking for new ideas, the act of branching out from the main subject in a 'holist' way allows you to see associations between activities, which can then trigger fresh ideas on the subject. Ideas emerge as a result of playing around with the available information. The Mind Map also allows you to introduce pictures or images as well as words, which in turn can produce new images about what may be possible. All this is very difficult, if not impossible, when working with lists or text.

The act of summarizing a business report is made much easier by highlighting key points, and identifying the main subject for transfer to a Mind Map. The same is true for intractable subjects such as conflict between two countries, or between two organizations. Explanation of such conflicts, in text, can be very difficult to follow, but diagramming as a Mind Map allows you to discover essential relationships which leads in turn to an uncovering of key points and a greater clarity in understanding.

BUSINESS PURPOSE OF THE MIND MAP

Before writing a report, or even making comments about something, map out your perception and ideas about what is involved, showing how they are related to each other. This leads to a more organized and thought-through presentation.

When discussing a problem, or an opportunity, with colleagues, a mapping of your ideas can be compared with their maps to produce a master picture of what can be done.

When needing to hold in memory information that includes complex relationships, a Mind Map on paper will provide an overall picture that can be more readily recalled than the same information in lists. This is one reason why many managers find this type of diagram very useful when preparing for a meeting.

When planning a marketing exercise or a sales promotion, the mapping of target areas and subjects can focus more exactly on what is to be done.

SUMMARY AND CONVENTIONS

In summary, a person needs to feel free to include anything in a Mind Map; the image ought to reflect spontaneous feelings as well as ideas that have been carefully thought through. The result is a unique map of the drawer's thinking. The real power of the diagram can be realized when it is possible to compare maps drawn by others, and build a shared understanding from the outcome.

Conventions for the Mind Map

- Use simple lines and/or arrows linking components.
- Include any components that come to mind.
- Do not consult others until the Mind Map has been completed.
- Still use a clear title to name diagram and subject.
- Addition of functions to describe components is not needed.
- Begin in the middle of a page and work outwards; it is always better to work with a page in 'landscape'.
- Write all words in block capitals and in such a way that they can be read in the same direction; see the example Mind Maps above.
- Use different colours to enhance different areas of the diagram.

5   Relationship and influence

Relationship

By 'relationship' we mean some kind of connection, but no more than that. Quite simply that people or things, 'components' in diagram terminology, are connected and can be related together in some way. The connections are not always obvious unless we have some method of capturing on paper what is a pattern of relationships. The relationships are normally picked up from reading, listening or observation and reflect someone's perspective of how things are in reality.

Explore this perception of relationships within a large clothing retail business, as in Figure 5.1. Does the overall pattern make sense or not? If the pattern is acceptable there may be detail that is seen as incorrect. Think first about the pattern of relationships, then more deeply about the reasons why lines of relationship are shown in some places but not in others. A good example is the 'gap' between designers and sales staff. Any relationship, should it exist, will be open to numerous questions.

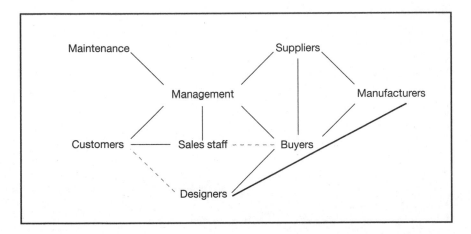

Figure 5.1   Relationship diagram of a large clothing retail business

This type of diagram is often called a spray or spider diagram. Unlike the Mind Map it is not necessarily unique to the person who is drawing it. In practice, for any given retail business, there must be a pattern of relationships in existence. How close Figure 5.1 is to reality would need to be established, but always in a particular context. The dotted lines reflect uncertainty about a relationship; some fashion designers for example do not appear to have any relationship with 'normal' people who are the most numerous customers. If the product was home furnishing a stronger relationship would be expected.

The person drawing the diagram is likely to have clear ideas about the relationships being shown, for example between management and buyers, and whether this relationship is any different when the retail business is part of a much larger retail chain. If the diagrammer wishes to communicate more detailed information about the relationship, whether it is about flow, influence, control or cause, then another type of diagram would be used. Further exploration, using other diagrams, would help greatly in clarifying any difficulties that can arise between these roles in a company.

Business application of the relationship diagram

At the level of project working in a particular company, a Relationship diagram can be drawn that would readily be recognized by many people in business.

Notice how open the diagram in Figure 5.2 is; it can take any shape, have any type of component whether people or things, and has no arrows to indicate direction of flow or influence of any kind. There are

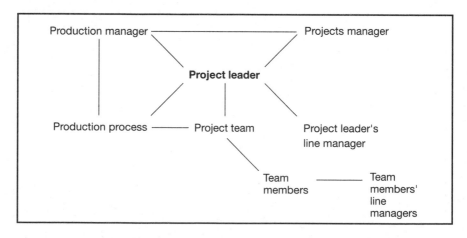

Figure 5.2 Relationship diagram of project working

no boxes or bubbles to contain groups of things, or any other symbols. The diagram shows a basic picture of how components are related to each other.

There is an interesting pattern to the diagram, showing at a glance a web of relationships that have a central focus. The exceptions are line managers, who feed into the web but who cannot be described as part of the overall interactions. Line managers who manage in flatter, matrix-type businesses can normally identify with such a diagram; even if it is not directly relevant to their own case they usually know of examples where 'outsider' relationships of this kind exist. Figure 5.3 shows a similar diagram for typical between-department relationships. A dotted line is used when the link is open to question, as between design and maintenance; often there is a declared aim to design for maintenance as well as production but the dotted line of uncertainty, again, is not untypical. Note how the pattern differs from the previous diagram in Figure 5.2.

A Mind Map drawn by someone in such a company, showing how he or she perceives between-department relationships, may well be different if the perception includes relationships that do not in practice exist, or lacks relationships that do exist. Getting near to reality is quite difficult, and a diagram can help establish a true pattern of actual relationships.

Some thought needs to be given to how components are described. There can be a relationship between a person and a non-animate object only if something can be done with the machine or equipment in question. For example, many people would find it difficult to think of a relationship between a person and a car other than through the functions of driving it from A to B, selling, buying or repairing. Without perform-

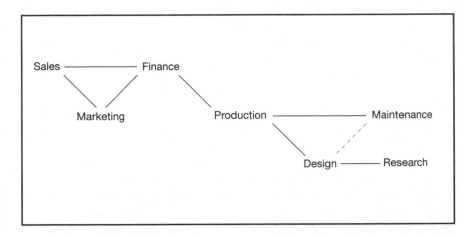

Figure 5.3 Relationship diagram of between-department relationship

ing a function the only thing a car can *do* is rust. To get around this problem we can elaborate on non-animate objects to help make the relationship clear. This point about clarity of wording is discussed, in Chapter 11, as one of the pitfalls of diagramming.

Business purpose of the relationship diagram

- Consider how many complex business problems are characterized by many different relationships between people, and between people and things. Use the diagram to illustrate in a holistic way the many relationships that exist, or could exist. The diagram provides an essential first step to understanding an existing pattern of relationships.
- Relationships can take many forms, as explained in this section, but before attempting to identify them, a Relationship diagram will show where they exist. The diagram then provides a means of directing attention to specific relationships.
- The gaps that can exist within a pattern of relationships, can go some way to explaining a difficulty. The diagram is a very effective way of highlighting gaps, where possibly much-needed relationships ought to exist.

Summary and conventions

In summary, this diagram shows where relationships exist, or where they do not exist when they should, and no more. Knowing this kind of information is an important first step in understanding complex situations. The components put into the diagram need to have their functions made clear. In the previous diagram, Figure 5.3, all components are stated as functions. In Figure 5.2, components such as 'Manager' or 'Team' have been qualified by the words 'production' or 'project' respectively.

The possibility of arriving at very different patterns of relationship should be seen as a prompt to our thinking. We can use the diagram to establish a consensus on where relationships do exist in practice. It is from this point that intervention is used to change the pattern of relationship if necessary. When making any change, it is wise to have a clear picture of the before-change state, and then develop the new pattern to a point where a comparison can be made between the two states.

Conventions for the Relationship diagram

- No arrows are used to show direction or influence.
- Give non-animate components some function.
- Any pattern of components is possible, depending upon a person's perception.
- Use a title to communicate the type of diagram and subject.
- Do not use boxes or blobs to group components, but go for simplicity.

Tree diagram

LINK TO RELATIONSHIP DIAGRAM

The Tree diagram is a natural extension of the Relationship diagram; the different configuration is simply a change to one that is hierarchical, but in practice this can have quite an impact on the way we think about the relationships. Suddenly, in a Tree diagram, more structure is introduced, dictated by the linear relationship of one component to another. Thinking back to the serialist and holist discussion in the introduction, the Tree, of all diagrams, comes closest to a drawing acceptable to the extreme serialist. There is an 'if A then B' order to the diagram that appeals to people who prefer to think in this way. Types of Tree diagram such as the objective Tree, logic Tree and organization chart all satisfy a felt need for preciseness and order.

The Tree diagram has a long history. One of the first recorded diagrams, the 'Tree of Porphyry', named after a third-century Syrian philosopher, was based upon the work of Aristotle. Even at that time the tree layout was seen as a very useful way to categorize information in a logical form, nature, then as now, providing the metaphor needed to describe human activity.

One diagram, the objective Tree shown in Figure 5.4, gives the image of a tree very well. There is, like the trunk, a central main objective to be achieved and it is this that feeds all other activity. Then there are what can be called sub-objectives, like branches, and for each sub-objective there can be various options available. Like leaves in full growth, some of these options will fall by the wayside when various advantages and disadvantages have been discussed. As an aid to thought it is a good idea to start an objective Tree by first agreeing on the key objective, then at least three possible sub-objectives, as shown in Figure 5.4. These key and sub-objectives state what has to be achieved. The options are purely about the 'how' of reaching these goals. The options prompt the question, 'How many ways can we reach this sub-objective?' The deliberations about options can often lead to the generation of further sub-objectives, or even the dropping of some existing sub-objective. The key objective could change too, but this is unlikely if it has been thoroughly agreed at the beginning. Since the various branches stem from this one key-objective decision, if this is changed then the whole process needs to begin again. The objective Tree is a very useful tool that enables us to think more clearly about what we mean by objectives.

AIMS AND OBJECTIVES

There tends to be confusion between aims and objectives in some written material, especially when the two are treated as alike. Think of an archer taking *aim*: this is what he or she does, but the *objective* is to either hit the target, hit the bull or score as highly as possible; the objective is measurable in some way while the aim is not. The measure may be quantitative, the archer scoring high, or qualitative, which could be developing the right style for archery. To be an objective a statement must be measurable in some way. It is this rigour in thinking that should be practised when working with the objective Tree. It is quite common to see objectives written as being things to be done, as activities, rather than things to be achieved. When reading any statement of objective the acid test is to ask, 'How do I measure that?'

Business application of the Tree diagram

An organization may state as an objective, 'to introduce a quality programme', but this is clearly an aim and not an objective, because 'introduce' is an activity and cannot be measured. However, the statement, 'to reduce wastage by 1 per cent', is an example of what needs to be achieved and is an objective statement. Once again we can see that the distinction is very real and is not just an example of playing with words.

When a key objective has been agreed as achievable, measurable and desirable, there are normally a series of sub-objectives or staging posts to be achieved on the way to realizing the ultimate goal. When thought has been given to describing each sub-objective, they can be added, as branches, to the central trunk. For each sub-objective there are normally a number of ways it can be achieved, that is, options for action. Techniques such as brainstorming, brainwriting, delphi or nominal group technique are useful ways to generate such options (see Craig, 1992 and Van Gundy, 1988), and these are added to extend the tree still further. This tree can be allowed to grow by adding to each option the advantages and disadvantages of following that particular route.

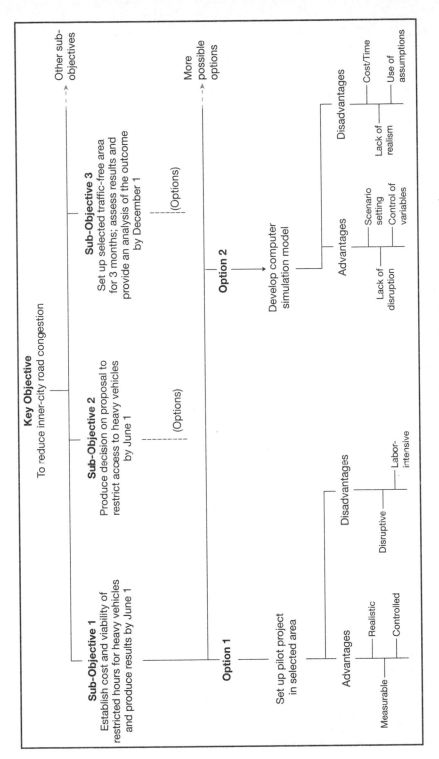

Figure 5.4 Objective Tree diagram to reduce road congestion

FAULTS AND CAUSES

Another use of the Tree diagram is to focus on faults and their causes. The fault Tree (Figure 5.5) is most commonly used in engineering, but has applications in insurance-claims investigation, accident investigation, declining sales, medicine and whenever symptoms, and causes of symptoms, are an area of concern.

Each observed symptom, such as machine failure, can have one or more faults associated with it. For each fault there can be one or more possible causes. Each cause normally has an optimum solution, or action to be taken. The same principle can be applied to other areas of business, mainly to clarify the real distinction between symptoms, faults and causes. A key objective when using this diagram (see Figure 5.6) is to locate the 'root cause or causes', the ultimate reason for the symptom being present.

All but one of the possible causes can realistically be linked to falling sales of a product. Motivation, on the other hand, can only ever be a symptom that needs further exploration. There are normally one or more critical events (faults) to contribute to poor motivation; for each fault there again can be one or more causes. The outcome here would be to develop a fault Tree for the symptom of poor motivation in this situation. The fault Tree is a very good vehicle for making us think deeply about the true nature of cause. The subject of cause will be picked up again in Chapter 7.

The need for more rigour in thinking, prompted by the drawing of objective and fault Trees, leads naturally to the idea of logic Trees. The next example (Figure 5.7) is quite common in public buildings where it is important to maintain emergency lighting and power supplies for safety purposes.

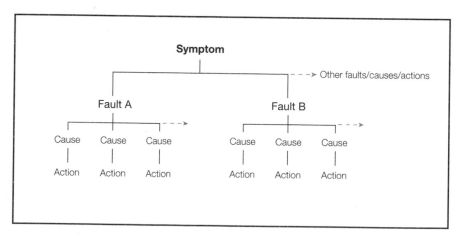

Figure 5.5   Fault Tree (outline)

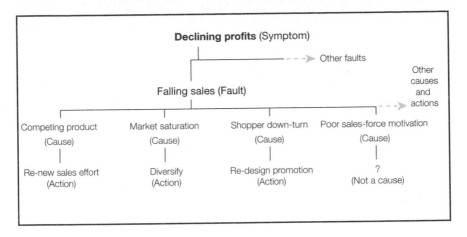

Figure 5.6 Fault Tree (sales related)

The diagram in Figure 5.7 is read bottom-up. The logic Tree, which could typically be of a hospital or hotel power supply, is based on two logic states, 'AND' and 'OR'. In digital electronics these are known as logic gates (there are many others such as NAND, NOR, NOT etc. which represent different logic states). There are also individual symbols to represent each of these states, but for the sake of simplicity we rely here upon plain boxes. Diagrams should be as simple as possible.

The logic diagram, as opposed to a digital circuit, has only two of these states. If, for example, there is an objective to be achieved and two actions are possible, the goal may be reached through either action, or may need to make use of both actions. The OR state in the diagram is

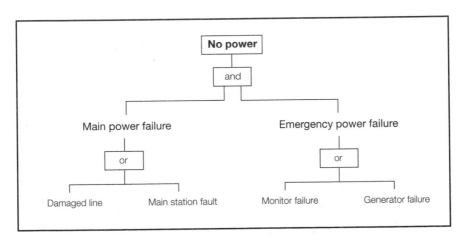

Figure 5.7 Logic Tree diagram of a complete power failure

saying that one action 'or' the other may be used. The AND state in the diagram is saying that one action 'and' the other are necessary to achieve the outcome. Being a tree layout, there can be a number of logic branches with links between them. The power failure Tree diagram in Figure 5.7 provides a simple example of these logic states in use.

OTHER TREE DIAGRAM USES

The diagram can be used for human activity in business too, such as summarizing the requirements for a particular job. The screening of large numbers of applicants can be a costly and time-consuming task; the logic Tree (Figure 5.8) is one useful way of reducing uncertainty in the process.

Where choice exists, the OR states are used and where no choice exists, the AND states are used. Looking at Figure 5.8, either analysis or programming skills are acceptable, and the same applies to degree or a higher diploma (HND). The AND states on the right-hand side show that both inputs must be satisfied at each step before going forward. Eventually a combination of choice and no-choice come together in one decision. Such a diagram when suitably extended can be used at the initial screening of applicants, to ensure that only candidates who meet the criteria are considered.

We come across examples of the Tree diagram when looking at organizational structure or at family trees. The typical organization chart shown in Figure 5.9 is a rather bland uninteresting picture, and repre-

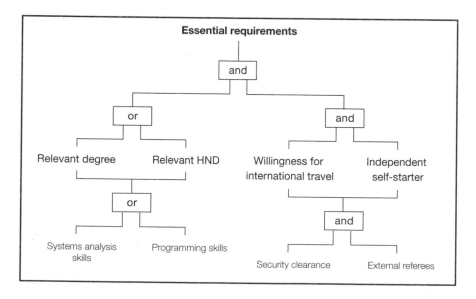

Figure 5.8   Job requirement logic Tree (brief example only)

sents one of the least dynamic diagrams available. The System Map and Influence diagram are more effective in describing an organization, or a department within an organization.

More interest can be added by superimposing an Influence diagram on top of the chart, or by turning it on its side – you could turn the book around now. Both variations provide different perspectives on the organization and again prompt our thinking. Combining the organization chart diagram with an Influence diagram is introduced in that section on influence (see Figure 5.12).

Business purpose of the Tree diagram

- Where relationships can be seen as linear or in hierarchical order, the Tree diagram provides the clearest overall picture. If the purpose is to establish objectives, use an objective Tree; if to show relationships in an organization, use an organization Tree, preferably with lines of influence added; if to locate causes of a problem, use a fault Tree.
- Think about how family relationships are shown in a family tree, and apply the same principle to any form of relationship. Sometimes

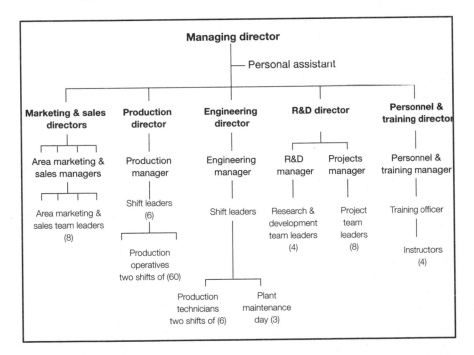

Figure 5.9 Typical organization tree diagram

the linking is by time, one thing following another in chronological order. Or the order can be logical as: if A *and* B then C; alternatively: if A *or* B then C.

Summary and conventions

In summary, the Tree diagram satisfies the need for some people to think in a linear and logical way. For those who are less logical the diagram can be combined with a Relationship or Influence diagram. The objective Tree is a very useful diagram, particularly during the early stages of a project, or when planning the development of a network Flow diagram, covered in Chapter 9.

Conventions for the Tree diagrams

- Where objectives are used it is critical that the main objective is clearly defined and valid.
- Objectives must be measurable in some way.
- An organization Tree diagram can be combined with an Influence diagram.
- The logic Tree makes use of two logic states.
- The fault Tree clarifies symptoms, faults and causes.

Influence diagrams

PEOPLE AND THEIR INFLUENCE

People or the roles they hold, may be said to carry influence – a major factor in business, where it can be demonstrated through persuasion, threat, charisma, causation or inducement. Sometimes influence is unconscious in so far as people achieve objectives through others without any deliberate effort. At other times influence comes from conscious effort, as in the case of political lobbyists acting on behalf of business. The links drawn on an Influence diagram show the existence of any kind of influence between the components shown on the diagram. There are different strengths of influence, as perceived by the people who experience or witness what is happening. These perceived strengths can be shown on the diagram by making lines of influence of different thickness. Here we build on the Relationship diagram, by saying that where connections are shown between two components, the link is one of influence rather than simply a relationship of some kind. It is not uncommon to hear people jump to conclusions about who is influencing whom, without taking time to think about the influence itself. When we are clear about where the influences are likely to be found, and have some idea about their relative strengths, then it is possible to go further and describe the *kinds* of influence. Again the diagram is being used as a very useful tool when colleagues are prompted to debate the lines of influence, their type and perceived strength. Some people link influence with cause; a certain kind of influence may be causal, but when talking about influence we cannot automatically assume causation. The result of someone's influence may be to make you think differently but not necessarily to act differently. Without activity of some kind, causation becomes very difficult to demonstrate clearly. Also, note from the section on the Relationship diagram that non-animate objects cannot really have any relationship except through the function they have been designed to perform; the same applies to influence. The function of the object, or what can be done, needs to be shown in the diagram. Look at 'Access to health records' in Figure 5.10: this 'access' aspect of health records can have some influence depending upon the extent of access, but not when simply stated as 'Health Records'. Health Records in themselves can have no influence, but remain in a file box or hard disk of a computer and do nothing until access is carried out.

To begin an exploration of this type of diagram, let us return to the General Practitioner's business.

Differences will be observed, when compared with a Relationship diagram. The arrows show direction of influence, from person A to person B, and an estimate of the relative strength of influence is shown by varying the thickness of arrows. Influence inevitably has some direction, from A to B, from B to A or in both directions. Some two-headed arrows are shown in the diagram like this, from one person to another:

Person A  Person B

Here, a reciprocal influence is being shown, A to B and B to A. This way of showing influence can only be valid when the strength of influence is judged to be equal in both directions. Where this equal situation does not exist, two arrows need to be used:

Person A   Person B

The Influence diagram is often supported by a short text, to elaborate further on each kind of influence, because more than one kind of influence can exist within the same Influence diagram. But remember that to illustrate particular kinds of influence such as cause or control within a

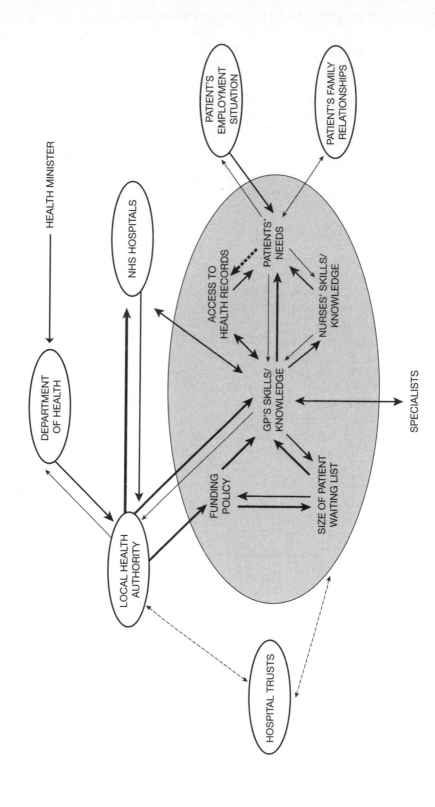

Figure 5.10 Influence diagram of a GP's practice

diagram, as opposed to describing them only in words, we need to use other types of diagram such as Multiple-Cause, Fishbone, Control, Flow etc. For example, in a Multiple-Cause diagram all links between components have causal influence.

Business application of the Influence diagram

In marketing the products or services of a business there can be much debate about the relevance of the mix of product, place, promotion, process, price, people and physical evidence – the 7Ps.

Figure 5.11 is an Influence diagram for marketing professionals to criticize, and possibly re-draw to include relative strengths of influence.

Observation of the marketing 7Ps indicates a mutual influence between the product, place where it is to be marketed, and people who are expected to buy. Price looks a bit out on a limb, and some professionals in marketing give it low priority on the assumption that if all other Ps have been managed well, price will have comparatively less influence. Promotion is influenced by the type of product and place; the influence of people on promotion could well be through place. This is a diagram that can promote considerable debate, and as this debate takes place the diagram is providing a catalyst for thinking about such marketing issues.

Looking back at the diagram in Figure 5.10, it is possible to speculate about the kinds of influence being exerted on the GP's business. For example, the GP has a 'controlling' influence over access to health records, and an 'expert' influence too. There is a two-way influence here because a strong 'dependency' exists between record information and the GP; without the influence of this information it would be very difficult for the GP to function in his or her role. There is an interesting two-way influence between GP and specialist; there could be two arrows

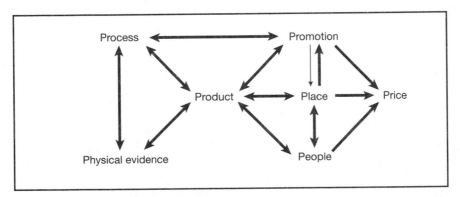

Figure 5.11   Influence diagram of marketing's 7Ps

here, because it is mainly 'expert' influence but at different levels of expertise. Influence diagrams can be interrogated like this to help us think more deeply about influence and ways of working.

There is one example in the diagram of one-way influence only, from funding policy to GPs. The perception here, rightly or wrongly, is that no influence exists in the reverse direction. If the component read as *amount* of funding the one- or two-way influence could be different. Simply, if the perception is of one-way influence only, then this is how it is shown.

Careful 'reading' of Influence diagrams can be quite revealing: sometimes a person may be shown, in a diagram, as being influenced quite strongly by one or more colleagues yet have no personal influence whatever elsewhere. This picture ought to raise questions about the function or purpose of this particular role.

If we consider the diagram of the GP's practice, it can be seen that funding of the practice has an influence, whereas some years earlier funding would not have existed in such a diagram. The impact of any new component like this can be followed through by developing a new diagram. We could also help our thinking by comparing diagrams of before and after the introduction of funding.

Dotted lines are shown because for the diagrammer the influence is unclear, and may be unclear to others as well!

Occasionally, a component in the environment can be said to influence everything within the boundary, and for this reason the arrow is drawn only to the boundary. In Figure 5.10 this type of arrow is from trust hospitals to the whole practice. But this arrow to the boundary is difficult to handle in a clear way because the strength of influence shown by the arrow is not likely to be the same for all contacts within the boundary. The direct influence to boundary, while acceptable in practice, is nevertheless rather vague and usually means there is room for much more thinking and discussion.

A strong influence is shown from 'Minister of Health' to 'Department of Health', when years ago this could be seen as minimal, so a comparison between earlier and later diagrams can lead to further questions, typically in this case about increased political involvement in health provision, and whether this ought to be encouraged.

From an initial reading of the diagram (remember that it is someone's perception), it is possible to see how major changes can be explored. Such a diagram can be used as before-after change analysis. Also, the impact of change in one part of a diagram can be followed through to check on possible impacts in other parts. How, for example, does the influence from funding policy relate to the influences between GP and specialist? The respective roles of people with regard to direction and strength of influence can also be explored. If we think of possible influences that could exist within the boundary shown on an Influence diagram, all or nearly all components ought to have influences on each other. When gaps, or no lines of influence, exist between components within a boundary it is likely that a problem of some kind is lurking within the system. For example, a diagram of this kind showing no lines of influence between access to health records and patients, as used to be the case, would indicate a problem, because both components are being seen as within the boundary and ought to have some linkage. Drawing an Influence diagram in the past would have made the gap between health records and patients, in terms of influence, more obvious.

Figure 5.9 in the section on Tree diagrams (p. 55) showed the conventional organization chart as a good example of branching and hierarchy, but as a rather uninspiring picture and limited as a diagram in its capacity to make us think. Figure 5.12 introduces the idea of superimposing an Influence diagram on the chart to produce a combined Influence-Tree diagram.

The organization Tree, or chart, takes on a rather different pattern of relationships, and could generate a good deal of thinking and debate about who influences whom and how. In this example, the personal assistant to the MD is seen as quite pivotal and a number of questions could be asked about influences with some managers but not with others. The MD is seen to have particular alliances that could be explored further. The personnel and marketing functions appear to be somewhat isolated from the main flow of influences. More lines of influence could be developed or in some cases removed as a result of exploring the diagram in detail. This exercise prompts thinking about how the structure actually operates, in contrast to the limited information provided by the standard organization chart as shown in Figure 5.9.

An Influence diagram of public transport provision is critically important to a business responsible for delivering this service. Drawing the diagram proves to be problematic, but this is simply reflecting the complexity of the situation. The influences that can dictate the direction of public transport provision are many and varied. The diagram in Figure 5.13 is simply an extract of a much larger picture. In this example the boundary (included in Figure 5.10) has been dropped to show an alternative way of presenting the Influence diagram. There are times when the boundary restricts the possibility of seeing the influence picture as one dynamic 'whole'. Drawing an Influence diagram with and without using the boundary is possibly the best way for someone to appreciate this point fully.

The strength of influence perceived between the various components provides possibly the biggest area of debate. Rather than simply 'who influences whom?' questions, the actual amount of influence becomes critical. After drawing this diagram and thinking about influence it is

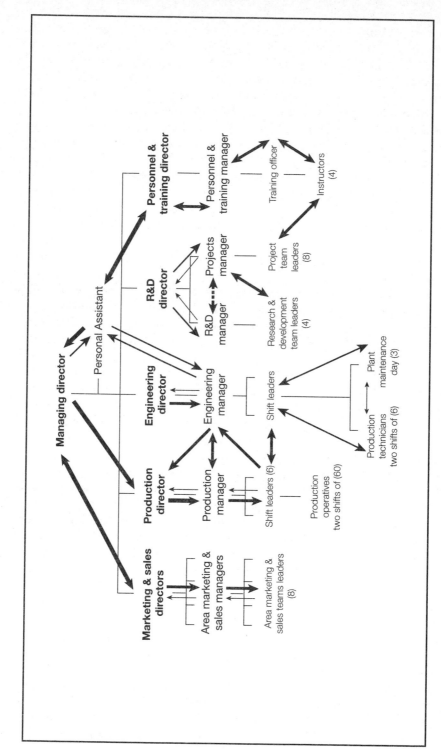

Figure 5.12 Organization Tree diagram with influences

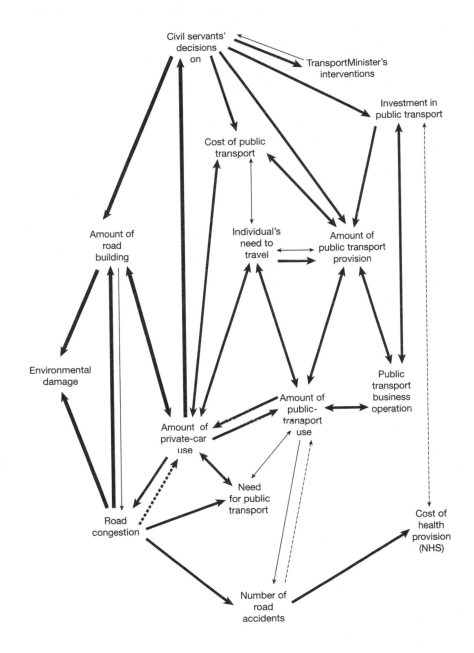

Figure 5.13 Influence diagram of public transport provision

difficult to see who or what influences the Transport Minister apart from contact with the civil service. Another possibility is influence from lobby groups on both the minister and the civil servants. Another issue that comes to mind from diagramming is whether the word 'policy' ought to be included, because from these deliberations there does not appear to be a policy.

There are a number of one-way influences where it is difficult to perceive any interactions taking place. It is also difficult to draw in public transport users' influence. To do this it is necessary to recognize a point of intervention where the public transport users' influence could be directed. The task of diagramming simply highlights such gaps in the pattern of influence. In short, the diagram reflects a mess and can be said to be close to reality. With all possible components and links drawn in, the picture would resemble a bowl of spaghetti. When drawing or reading Influence diagrams, look for the existence of 'tails' – components out on a limb which have no arrows leaving them. Sometimes this is inevitable, because to develop an arrow may mean going into another area of influence completely. One question to ask of 'tails' is, 'If no influence, why is it here?' 'Environmental damage' and possibly 'cost of health provision' are two 'tails' in this diagram that have relevance yet no obvious influence on other components, but do extend to have wider influence elsewhere.

The need to travel is an issue at the centre of this problem, and reducing its influence could have a significant impact upon other parts of the diagram.

Business purpose of the Influence diagram

- A useful approach is to begin with a System Map to establish the relative position of components, and then develop arrows of influence as shown in Figure 5.10. This two-stage or building approach helps people in business see where the key influences exist either in the whole organization or in one area.
- Initially, it helps to draw the arrows in lightly; then after thinking about influence, or discussing with others, fill in the different thickness for each arrow to show relative strengths. This thinking with diagrams satisfies a need in business to stand back from time to time so as better to understand what is happening.
- Think about how to describe the actions of someone, or something, that can be said to have an influence, so as to give more clarity to the diagram. Simply naming people or their role can be a way of

showing influence, which in this case could come from a certain kind of power or charisma – effectively an unconscious influence.

SUMMARY AND CONVENTIONS

In summary, the Influence diagram is serving its purpose when ideas are being generated about the subject. The diagram is normally drawn with much use of pencil and eraser or pen and whiteboard rubber. Drawing and re-drawing the diagram is one of the best ways to stimulate thinking about influences within an organization and, even more important for survival, make clear the business influences that exist outside the organization.

Conventions for the Influence diagram

- Use arrows to show direction of influence, either as one-way or two-way.
- Draw two arrows where different strengths of interaction need to be shown.
- Use varying thickness of arrows to show estimated and comparative strength of influences.
- Non-animate objects cannot have influence in themselves (it is what they are capable of doing that creates the influence), so their function or what they do needs to be stated.
- People can have influence simply by being. (But acknowledge that this could be a philosophical issue.)
- Any influence arrow to a boundary calls for more debate.
- The use of a boundary is optional; a good idea is to diagram influences with and without a boundary to check which outcome best meets your perspective.

6   Control in business

Input-output (I/O) diagram

The Input-Output diagram is based on the principle of the black box similar to those searched for after an air accident. The black box flight recorder has inputs and as the result of a process inside the box produces outputs. The actual process within the box must be trusted to perform as it was designed to do. The critical variables are to be found as inputs and outputs, and this type of diagram concentrates only on these variables. An everyday example is baking a cake at home; there are inputs, then a baking process, and an output. In this case the oven acts as the black box and apart from adjusting certain inputs, the heat setting or timing, there is little that can be done to influence the baking process. Whether the output pleases or does not please largely depends upon how the inputs are handled. When using I/O diagrams, it is the inputs and outputs that we are primarily concerned about. When an error is experienced at the output side (in our example this could be an inedible or burnt cake), it is almost certain that the cause of the problem lies with one or more of the inputs. When no cause can be found among the inputs, then a process-type cause could exist – in this case possibly a faulty oven.

Figure 6.1 shows a domestic version of this baking task. As pointed out earlier, this and most other diagrams are not definitive. If this were a commercial cake then we would add the 'cost of materials' and 'cost control' as inputs, and match this with a second output entitled 'cost-effective production'. There can be as many outputs as required; most I/O diagrams have fewer outputs than inputs but at times they may be equal in number, and in certain chemical processes outputs exceed inputs.

Business application of the I/O diagram

The outputs need to reflect the inputs. There is no point in having 'effective performance' as an output if there is no input that enables you to

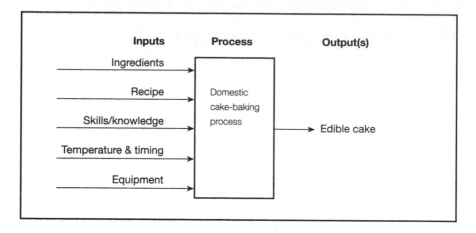

Figure 6.1   Input-Output diagram of domestic cake baking

achieve this. If in our cake example, the output was stated as 'a cake to a specific standard', rather than simply 'edible cake', then 'quality control' or 'quality assurance' is needed as an input.

Commercial baking is a different process, so an I/O diagram will look different (Figure 6.2). The additional inputs and outputs, included here, encourage us to ask questions about standards of performance or the *effectiveness* of cake production. In contrast, when thinking about *efficiency*, we can ask whether the outputs could be achieved with fewer inputs, or at least with less of a specific input. In other words, we are asking how to achieve more with less, to improve the efficiency. Seeing the links between inputs and outputs in this way allows us to generate questions, and at times ideas, about such issues as appropriateness, effectiveness, efficiency or suitability.

Another useful application of I/O diagrams is to check whether people are clear about the purpose of a process. What is this process? What is it doing? These may seem simple questions until you ask people to agree on what to write inside the black box and to define the inputs and output(s) clearly. Here, the simple I/O diagram becomes a very useful way for a group of people to clarify various and possibly conflicting ideas about a process or, in particular, a new business initiative.

It is normal to draw I/O diagrams for quite specific processes such as buying, baking, building or marketing. It would be possible to draw such a diagram for an organization as large as IBM or BT – all of it! A black-box description could be 'BT's business process'. The outcome would be a diagram so large that it would go beyond what could really serve any useful practical purpose. However, a more focused I/O diagram for 'BT business account sales process' would have a practical purpose of making you think in this way about a more specific function.

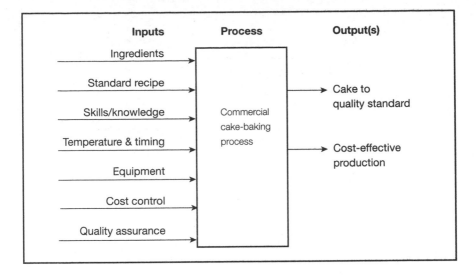

Inputs	Process	Output(s)
Ingredients		
Standard recipe		Cake to quality standard
Skills/knowledge	Commercial cake-baking process	
Temperature & timing		Cost-effective production
Equipment		
Cost control		
Quality assurance		

Figure 6.2 Input-Output diagram of commercial cake baking

For example, what could be added, removed or modified to improve efficiency or effectiveness of sales? Could there be other outputs? Any new thoughts about the actual process? Questions of this kind, arising out of an I/O diagram, can bring about productive changes.

We could be forgiven for thinking that the next example of an I/O diagram is definitive and beyond any need for change. Increasingly, the performance of a hospital operating theatre is seen in business terms, with control of effectiveness and efficiency a major issue. This I/O diagram of lucid patient identification for operating theatre admission provides food for thought and should be of some interest to all of us. A diagram of this kind can help in the deliberations that are part of making such a process foolproof or fail-safe. All possible eventualities can be covered by making sure that all necessary inputs are in place, and in such a way that they cannot fail. As explained earlier, the title of the diagram is very important too: here the word 'lucid' is critical. For non-lucid patients, such as those from accident/emergency entry, the inputs need to change to take account of the fact that the patient cannot be questioned.

This particular process does still fail from time to time, leading to a successful and correct operation but the wrong patient, or a successful but wrong operation, for example. When such errors occur, it shows that failing-safe has not yet been achieved and more work needs to be done.

A different I/O diagram is needed in cases where the correct patient has been identified but the wrong operation performed. Here we are thinking about a different process. The diagram black box would need to be described as 'Operating theatre procedures process'. The message is

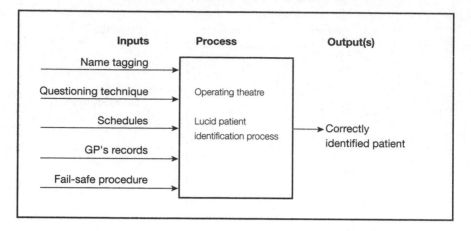

Figure 6.3   Input-Output diagram of operating theatre lucid patient identification

that an I/O diagram is focused on a specific process, and it is important to be clear about the nature of this process.

A good starting point when thinking about processes that fail, is to ask what an I/O diagram for a particular failed process looks like, and how it differs from one that has never failed. Comparisons between diagrams of failed and not-failed processes can be a useful tool for learning. We will revisit this hospital example in the next part dealing with Control-loop diagrams.

To pick up again on the theme of public transport provision, an I/O diagram, though simple in outline, does need a good deal of thought when faced with this particular process. There is a temptation to include as inputs many more elements such as car use, road building or shopping patterns. The process described in the black box disciplines us to focus on actual inputs relevant only to providing this kind of transport.

In Figure 6.4 we have this clear perspective on the process; it shows the bare bones of what is essential about this kind of use of public transport, and we need to keep it in mind as the subject begins to become more complex. The overall subject of achieving more effective and efficient use of public transport contains a number of related I/O diagrams dealing separately with different processes such as routeing, costing and fares, maintenance, and fleet selection. Using a number of I/O diagrams in this way allows us to compare different factors and understand how they relate to each other.

BUSINESS PURPOSE OF THE I/O DIAGRAM

- Think carefully, in a very specific way, about the actual process you

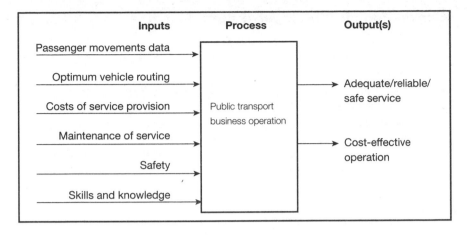

Figure 6.4 Input-Output diagram of public transport
business operation

are dealing with; this is not as obvious as it sounds. The words to go into the black box must contain a verb or a verbal noun to describe how the inputs are being converted to outputs. The purpose here is to think of a business as a transformation process, taking some initial inputs and converting them to useful and appropriate outputs. Processes, or the way things are done, tend to remain intact for long periods. When inputs change it is necessary to consider the possible impact upon the process, and subsequently upon the output(s).

- Make effective use of the diagram by challenging any assumptions about the inputs, and the output(s). Any redundant activity? Any new development that could be included? Are output(s) or inputs ready for change? And so on, until you are satisfied that the diagram reflects a true state and is one that needs little improvement.

SUMMARY AND CONVENTIONS

The Input-Output diagram is much more focused than the Influence diagram produced on public transport provision in Figure 5.12. The two diagrams offer different perspectives on the subject, yet are complementary. Where specific processes can be identified within an Influence diagram, then appropriate I/O diagrams can be developed. An I/O diagram is a very useful tool for clarifying ideas about a process, its essential inputs and how to state the desired outputs in a concise way. The diagram also prompts questions about how effective or how efficient each input could be.

Conventions for the Input-Output diagram

- Always include arrows to show direction of flow from input, through the process, to output.
- The actual process is named in the black box and must contain a verb or verbal noun to state how the inputs are transformed into outputs. You cannot have simply the name of a department or company – the actual process must be included.
- Each input must be seen to play a part, and be reflected in at least one output. Each output must have at least one input related to it. In other words, each output must be seen to emerge from an input or from a combination of inputs.
- The title of the diagram must include the fact that it is an Input-Output diagram and state the process, e.g. 'Input-Output diagram of operating theatre lucid patient identification'.
- Each I/O diagram must be for a specific process: patient identification is such a process. The actual operation in the theatre is a different process and would require a different I/O diagram or possibly more than one.

Control diagram

Problems caused by lack of control are common enough and examples can be enormously varied, from poor control (or lack of control) of crowd entry at football matches to pension dealings. A frequently asked question when control problems arise is, 'Who was in control?' An equally important question, but heard less often, is, 'How was the control designed and organized?' A Control diagram can help bring answers to both questions, and go beyond this by encouraging us to think about the true nature of control. What are the essential features of control? What types of control are available? Controlling for what? These and other questions come to mind when developing a Control diagram.

In textbooks or articles you may come across quite wide variations on the standard diagram used here, but you will often find that one or more essential control features are missing. The standard core diagram given in this section contains all features necessary for effective control.

Control at its most basic level is associated with mechanical or electric/electronic processes such as controlling engine speed, furnace temperature or railway signalling. Control diagramming has gone beyond these applications to include control that involves human behaviour. In 1995, a Bank of England report into the collapse of Barings Bank stated: 'The true position was not noticed earlier by reason of a serious failure of controls and management confusion within Barings'. A debatable point is whether the statement ought to have read as *lack* of controls rather than *failure* of controls.

An initial attempt to spark off thinking and debate about the nature of control at the Bank could look like the diagram in Figure 6.5. You should be able to recognize the embedded Input-Output diagram, with seven key inputs being transformed into one 'bottom-line' output. The black box contains the daily processing of Barings' Futures in Singapore. Now, the introduction of control feedback to this I/O diagram brings in other diagram features of:

- actuator;
- environmental influences;
- sensor;
- feedback;
- comparator; and
- goal.

The *actuators* cover tasks or methods that need to be adopted when any correction or modification to an input is necessary.

The *environmental influences* are those that may be beyond control but that can seriously interfere with even the most efficient control process. When baking a commercial cake, the process is normally under the total control of the people involved. This is not the case for managing more complex operations such as futures, or maintaining railway signalling. It is just as necessary to know what cannot be controlled as it is to know what is being controlled.

The *sensor* can be a device such as a temperature probe, or it can be a named person; in the example above, a question mark serves the purposes of investigation and debate very well. The sensor, whether mechanical or human, needs clear criteria for knowing what is to be the standard of performance from the output.

The *feedback* can be either negative or positive. The main credit for developing the concept of feedback goes to M. Maruyama (1963). When discussing negative feedback we use an earlier meaning of the word 'negative' which meant correcting or maintaining stability, rather than the modern meaning of being somehow 'bad' or 'unwelcome'. If we wish to maintain a room at near constant temperature then negative feedback is used to reduce the heat input when the temperature rises and to increase the heat input when the temperature falls. When we wish for ongoing increases in the output, having higher and higher bonus payments in the Barings example, we use positive feedback. Engineering processes tend to use negative feedback, unless the subject is higher

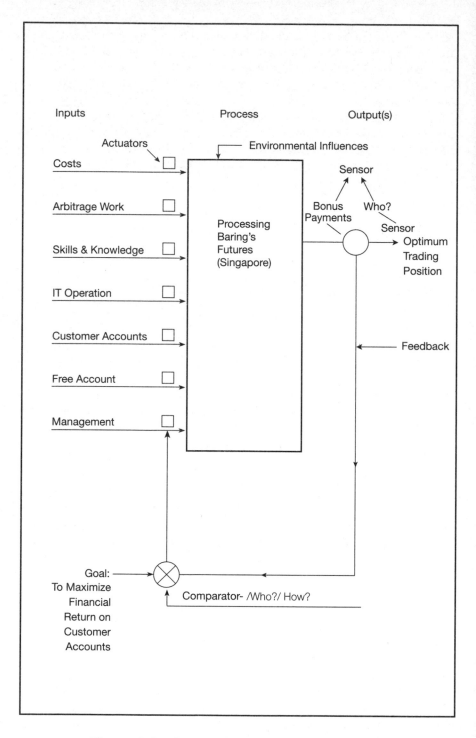

Figure 6.5 Control diagram of futures processing

quality, and sales managers look for positive feedback on most occasions. A sales manager, acting as a comparator, needs to, activate still further the input that led to increased sales output. Again, depending upon perception, we may seriously question the use of positive feedback if we feel a need for limits to growth – in other words, if we take account of the view that we cannot continue to produce more and more goods and services if the world's resources are to be sustained over the long term.

To summarize, negative feedback acts on the inputs by increasing or decreasing in order to *maintain* a desired result at the output. Positive feedback acts on the inputs in order to *maximize* results at the output.

Like the sensor, the *comparator* can be a device or a named person. The comparator compares the standard from the output with the overall goal of the process and triggers off any changes to one or more inputs. The sensor gives only the actual outcome from the process. The goal on the other hand normally reflects a longer-term view. For example, a person acting as sensor would test a repaired aircraft engine to the standards of effective and efficient operation which would also be part of the goal, but he or she could not test for reliability, which would also be part of the goal, because the engine needs to be in use for a longer period to discover how reliable it is. If after some time it is discovered that reliability has fallen short of the goal, then the feedback comes into operation to discover where, or if, the problem lies within this particular area of control. In the case of immediate problems, the goal is compared with the output. When the comparator finds a discrepancy between the output and the goal then action needs to be taken, through the actuators, to correct or modify one or more inputs.

BUSINESS APPLICATION OF THE CONTROL DIAGRAM

These features of control and their operation, as described here, were largely absent from the Barings case – hence my questioning whether there was a failure of control or no control at all. A Control diagram, such as the one shown here, can be done in around thirty minutes of thinking and drawing time. A diagramming exercise like this at Barings would undoubtedly have highlighted major weaknesses in the operation of this futures process.

Something can be learned from most failures by examining the method of control in this way: Chernobyl, King's Cross, Clapham or Three Mile Island are typical examples that come to mind. However useful this retrospective learning may be, the real value in diagramming of this kind is in designing and planning to ensure that effective control is in place that will go some way to avoid failure in the future.

Now let us revisit the operating theatre, considered earlier, to see how this idea of control could be applied there. A key issue here (see Figure

6.6) is whether the feedback is desirable in a situation where serious errors at the output cannot be tolerated under any circumstances. If we remove the feedback loop then what is called open-loop control exists. An open-loop Control diagram implies that the control is carried out at the input side rather than at the output. The design of the identification method has to be totally foolproof, and it is this method that operates at the point of input.

The traditional inspector, placed at the end of a production line, who returned faulty goods back to the input, where a supervisor acts as a comparator, is a practical example of closed-loop control. A different approach is to remove the inspector and build quality into the process at the input to ensure quality at the output. This is an example of open-loop control. When an error does occur, there is an inquest and every effort is made to avoid a repetition of the problem. In a process controlled in an open-loop way no feedback exists to allow for repeat circuits of the same problems.

Although manufacturing is used as an example here, the idea of open and closed-loop control applies to a wide range of human activities. In the service industry a survey of existing customers about existing products can be seen as an example of closed-loop control. It is doubtful whether dealers in Rolls Royce cars would send such a survey to their customers because it is expected that quality will be built in up to the point of delivery.

The situation is rather different during the launch of new products or services where feedback can be most valuable. Whenever a Control diagram is used in this way the aim is to establish best practices at the beginning through the inputs so that open-loop control can operate as far as possible once the product or service has been adopted.

Most processes in the health services need to be of the open-loop type if errors are to be avoided as opposed to being corrected. When thinking about control being used with human activity it has to be acknowledged that closed-loop control is effectively an error system: without error the loop does not come into action so, logically, closed-loop control depends upon error for its existence. The situation is different when controlling railway signals or the temperature in a room automatically: then the closed-loop performs a very necessary function.

Having made these points about human activity and closed-loop diagramming there is a particular use of the loop that can be of value, which is often referred to as double-loop learning.

The well-known marketing story comes to mind of a customer buying a drill when he or she does not really want a drill, but a hole in a wall. An organization making drills could usefully ponder from time to time on their goal of being the world's finest drill manufacturer. Their revised goal could well be to provide the most effective means of making holes,

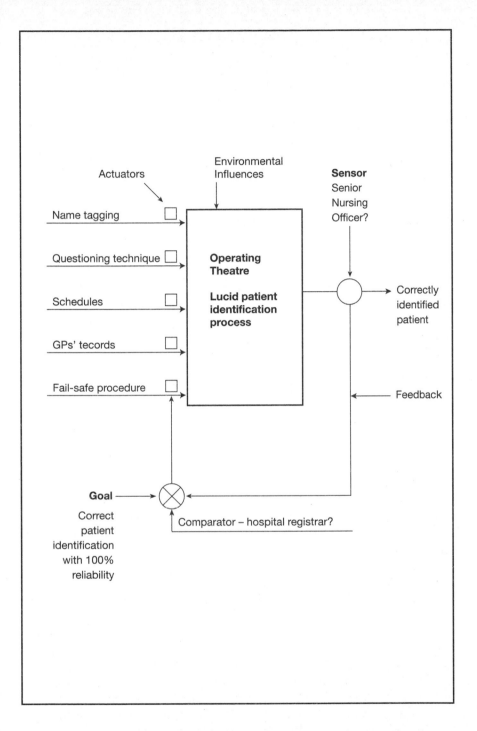

Figure 6.6 Control diagram of operating theatre patient identification

as illustrated in Figure 6.7. With this goal, they would be open to learning and responsive to any new ideas such as using a laser gun or some other, as yet not thought of, way to make holes.

The single feedback loop to the production manager, in the upper half of the diagram, implies that this is how we do things around here: we have our process, its inputs and outputs, our clear standards, and we know where we are going – the goal. However, nothing can change in this single closed-loop diagram without also influencing all other parts. If the goal remains fixed, then by definition all other parts are relatively fixed too. People in organizations who are prepared to learn, and go on learning, regularly examine their overall goals with the possibility of changing them. In management jargon the term 'learning organization' is used to describe this approach.

The Swedish company Silva have produced navigation compasses for many years, but were quick to adopt the possible replacement by selling Global Positioning Systems (GPS) that make use of American satellites to fix positions at ground level. The new system may never totally replace the need for conventional compasses but if it does, the original makers should not suffer. In contrast, many shipbuilders around the world closed when an alternative goal of being best steel fabricators, rather than builders of best ships, would have given them more flexibility. Making use of a double-loop diagram helps us think about how flexible our goals can be, and how many alternative goals are possible. When this type of thinking is in place change becomes part of everyday work and ceases to be a major issue. This principle of looking at single-loop ways of working, and periodically going into double-loop mode, provides one route to being more innovative.

Most double-loop diagrams take the second loop from an extension of the feedback line from the sensor, shown with a dotted line in the diagram, when in reality it is the person or persons acting as the comparator who would normally evaluate any new goals against existing goals.

When it has been decided to change a goal, then changes must be made elsewhere in this diagram, as well as taking account of the various influences that exist outside the black box and beyond the scope of the inputs. Effectively, a new diagram would be produced.

The control of a public transport business begs many questions, but the essential control features can be captured within a diagram. An important consideration here is that a number of influences 'bombard' the black box from outside which can be beyond the control of the business. As noted earlier, what can be controlled should be controlled effectively, and what cannot be controlled should be known about.

When discussing the Influence diagram for transport provision in Figure 2.12 some difficulty was experienced in locating transport users'

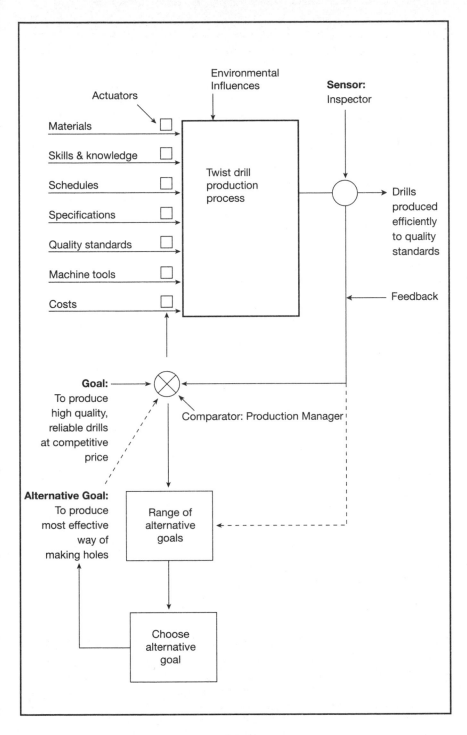

Figure 6.7 A double-loop learning diagram

influence. This ought to feature as an input to this Control diagram (Figure 6.8), but in practice is not really there. Contact with the public provides the main source of information to the sensor, and it is this information that is acted upon, but this is after the process has taken place. The outcome is that closed-loop control is in operation most of the time. The control model is very effective at highlighting how reactive a business is towards events, as opposed to being more proactive.

The ideal situation would be one where needs were established at the input by taking into account passenger, general public and environmental requirements. The process should be designed to satisfy these needs in a way that allowed for open-loop control. Unfortunately this is not the case; feedback is constantly in use to help satisfy an ongoing debate about what provision ought to be achieved, which gives an indication of the amount of error that is built into the process. There are numerous passes around the loop to correct problems. Reasons for this situation will be explored later by using other diagrams.

BUSINESS PURPOSES OF THE CONTROL DIAGRAM

- Whenever the subject of control is raised, a good idea is to draw a Control diagram, involving if possible colleagues who ask questions like 'Who is in control around here?' or, 'Is this project out of control?' A well-thought-through diagram will clarify a situation enormously.
- When planning a new job, task or project, one Control diagram, or if necessary more, should be drawn as a standard part of preparation. This activity will go a long way to avoid problems of control later.
- When any kind of failure has been experienced, the drawing of a Control diagram normally raises problems of control if control did in fact exist. Often failure of control is given as an explanation for problems in business, but if a Control diagram had been applied, it could possibly have been shown that no real control existed.

SUMMARY AND CONVENTIONS

In summary, the Control diagram is a logical extension of the Input-Output diagram and uses the same 'black-box' principle. The diagram helps us be clear about the distinction between positive and negative feedback, and how this can help our thinking about the nature of control. Whenever possible, in processes dictated by people rather than machines, open-loop control ought to be the aim. In mechanical or electrical systems the closed loop plays a vital role.

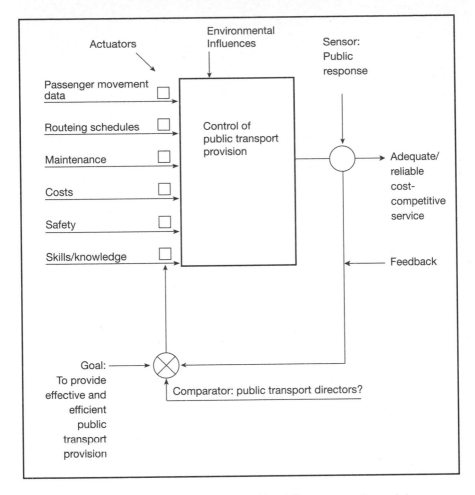

Figure 6.8 Control diagram of public transport provision

Conventions for the Control diagram

- Include all arrows as shown in the examples given here.
- Think carefully about the inputs to be included and how they match output(s).
- Indicate when there are influences beyond the black box.
- Show the sensor and indicate what measure is to be used.
- State clearly the overall goal, which must embrace the output but which is likely to include longer-term features.
- Show who or what will play the role of comparator.

7   Thinking about causation

Multiple-cause diagram

A line from a humorous TV series, *'You rang my Lord?'*, comes to mind when thinking about causation: 'There's a mongoose under your bed!' 'Yes, that is to keep the snakes away.' 'But it is stuffed!' 'Yes, but the snakes do not know that.' The absence of snakes was being taken to be the consequence of having a stuffed mongoose on guard. Put another way, the presence of that animal was, alone, a necessary cause of being free of snakes. Lady Agatha, who was in the bed, was known for very eccentric behaviour, but in real life there can be equally muddled thinking about the nature of causation.

When, for example, there is a consequence B because action A has made it happen, we can say that A has caused B. This could hardly be simpler, yet there is much confusion and misunderstanding about causation. People, especially in politics, argue endlessly about causal links such as those that could exist between poverty and crime, unemployment and crime, pollution and poor health, car use and pollution, or a particular kind of television watching and violence. Many politicians, and people in public life generally, appear to have a confused concept of causation. Much discussion that is heard, or reported, shows a lack of understanding about the true nature of what is happening when something is said to be a cause. The same comment can be applied to people who have to deal with causation as a critical part of their work – for example, maintenance engineers, lawyers or medical practitioners.

One of the difficulties arises because causation is seldom a simple one-way process. The simple single-causal relationship of B being the consequence of A, such as a taxi stopping when you wave your hand in the street, is not so common. Trying to find and explain the cause of events in most human activity often involves several possible causes. Yet this does not adequately explain the confusion over what is and what is not *causal*, because even in the case of many causes each cause needs to be clearly identified and justified as being truly causal. The basic idea of having necessary or sufficient cause is not always grasped, and the interaction between symptom, fault, cause and ultimate cause goes largely unnoticed. These features of causation will first be explored by using the Multiple-Cause diagram, then by using the Fishbone and finally the Sign diagram.

The first point to note in drawing this type of diagram is that each statement must be an action of some kind. A person or a machine without some kind of action cannot cause anything: it is what the person *does* or how the machine is *used* that is or is not causal. Therefore it is important to be clear about the action that is said to cause, rather than supposing the outcome to be a result of some other kind of influence. Yet we hear politicians say that 'the Chancellor' has caused a drop in the pound. This may, in some cases, be a form of shorthand meaning 'the Chancellor's actions', but often this is attributing cause to a place or person where it cannot belong.

There are times when cause is shown in a flow-like way, but this cannot be correct, because flow cannot be causal. We can say that if A is always a precursor to all occurrence of B, then, in this case, A is a necessary cause. This does not mean causal, because A comes *before* B in a flow-like way. At a simple level we can say that lunch follows breakfast but is not caused by breakfast. In an assembly plant, painting may follow assembly but one does not cause the other.

Another quite common area of confusion is when an event coincides with another event and one is said to cause the other. An example of this was provided by deaths at an English football ground. The actions that led to overcrowding were said to cause the deaths, but this was not true. These actions, said to be by police, should have caused the crowd to spill over to the playing area, and in turn caused the stopping of the game. The deaths were caused by having fences that stopped the inevitable over-spill. Such problems in thinking are due to confusing two separate but related events. The overcrowding was one problem, but the deaths were essentially separate in terms of causation. The two outcomes, overcrowding and deaths were related (Relationship diagram) but the relationship was not causal. The necessary cause of the deaths was quite clearly the rigid design of the fencing. One solution to be introduced was total seating and the removal of spectator standing, but, standing does not cause crowd deaths, so still the confusion goes on. The idea of what is causal needs careful thought, and drawing a Multiple-Cause diagram helps greatly in getting more insight into this seemingly obscure subject. Before looking in detail at a diagram, it is helpful to summarize the distinction between sufficient and necessary cause:

- If action A always results in B, then A can be said to be a *sufficient* cause of B. But B could happen without A and be caused in a number of different ways. In other words, the fact that A always leads to B, does not mean that B cannot happen without A.

- If A is *always* a precursor to any occurrence of B, then A can be said to be a *necessary* cause of B. Occurrence B would not exist without A being present, even though other conditions may have to be present as well.

When the possible cause of lung cancer is discussed it is almost certain that cigarette smoking will come first into people's minds. However, while such smoking is recognized as a contributory cause of the problem, it cannot be called either a sufficient or a necessary cause. (See the definition of sufficient and necessary causes above.) To be a sufficient cause the occurrence of smoking (A) would always lead to the cancer (B). To be a necessary cause, smoking would always be the precursor to lung cancer. Neither, however, is the case. The activity of smoking can be a cause when added to, or in combination with, other possible causes that may or may not be sufficient or necessary causes. If someone had within them a necessary cause of the disease such as genetic disposition then you could argue that their smoking can do comparatively little further harm. Another view is that smoking may not lead to the disease at all if carried out in a less polluted environment. Such debate can be quite controversial, and one way to gain an overall picture of what is a highly complex subject is to produce a Multiple-Cause diagram, as shown in Figure 7.1. An important point to note about this diagram is the web-like pattern that is produced. This rather complex interaction is a feature of causation. If each event simply followed a previous event in sequence, written either horizontally or vertically down the page, it would be a flow of some kind such as the order of different processes in a factory and would be unlikely to show causation.

When drawing Influence diagrams it is possible to show perceived strengths by varying thickness of line, but it is difficult to justify this approach with Multiple-Cause diagrams. When the influence is causal it is generally sufficient to draw all links as being of the same strength. Cause is cause is cause, and it can only be understood clearly by looking at two events at any one time, then at another two events, and eventually at a spider-web type of picture. In Figure 7.2 we have A said to cause B, then B said to be a cause of C, then B and C contributing to passive smoking.

In this development of the lung cancer Multiple-Cause diagram the strength of the causal influence of cigarette smoking can only be judged in terms of a contribution to a certain type of air pollution, which is then part of general pollution and both together lead to passive smoking. The strength of the causal influence is very difficult to make as a direct link to the disease – or is it? By asking questions that have been prompted by

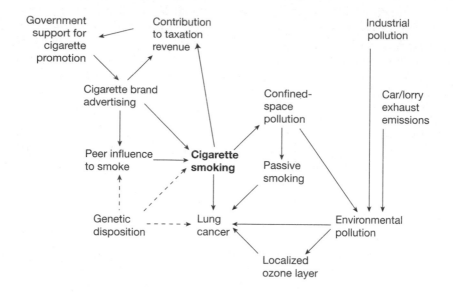

Figure 7.1   Multiple-Cause diagram of lung cancer

the drawing we have yet another example of the diagram doing its job as a tool for thought.

The possible cause labelled 'genetic disposition' in the Multiple-Cause diagram of lung cancer, if proved, would be an example of necessary cause; whenever this cause (A) exists, then the disease (B) will occur. The dotted line indicates possible causal link but without sufficient sound evidence. The perception of some people could lead them to draw the diagram with all lines being dotted, to indicate their level of uncertainty.

This type of diagram can be used whenever the cause of 'good' or 'bad' events needs to be adequately explained. It is much more common for the diagram to be used whenever there is a 'problem', but it is equally valuable for explaining success, so that lessons can be learned about how and why things occur as they do to bring about that success.

BUSINESS APPLICATION OF MULTIPLE-CAUSE DIAGRAM

The next example of a Multiple-Cause diagram (Figure 7.3) considers the factors that could cause a group of people to become a successful team. When could a successful group be called a successful team? Much is written about team-building in business, so there must be an assumption that a 'team' is in some way different from a 'group'.

There are a number of possible causal influences that can lead to what is perceived to be a successful team. One interpretation of this diagram (or perception) is that an ultimate cause exists. Without equal and shared

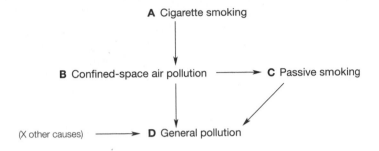

Figure 7.2   Extract from lung cancer multiple-cause diagram

accountability a group of people cannot really be said to function as a team; this is saying that here we have a *necessary* cause. A group of people cannot become a successful team (B) without a causal link of equal and shared accountability (A). There are many collections of people called teams where this necessary cause does not exist, and these become known generally as pseudo-teams. This statement itself can be a sufficient cause of consternation because if applied rigorously there would be many groups of people throughout business and industry, but very few teams. With each 'causal' link we need to ask whether A (tail of arrow) can cause B (head of arrow) to occur, or can B exist without A?

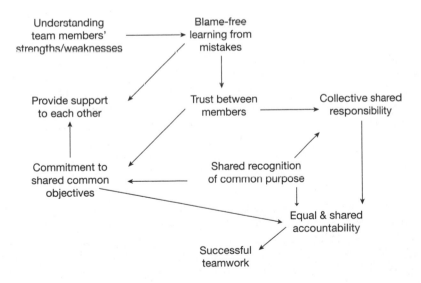

Figure 7.3   Multiple-Cause diagram of successful teamwork

Asking what causes public transport provision may well be of interest, but does not get us very far in understanding the issues surrounding this subject. Instead, we need to focus on problems or on positive examples to help explain what can be causing one or the other. Some people do not recognize the need for more than a very basic provision of public transport and would argue for a reduction of services and a decline in the business. What causes people to arrive at this view? In beginning to draw the diagram it is a good idea to begin by writing a statement of the subject being caused at the bottom of our large sheet, and then to practise what can be called backward thinking. How many causes can be directly linked to this subject? Then, what events lead to these causes or how many other causal links can we identify? By working backwards in this way it is sometimes possible to arrive at what can be described as a root cause: a fundamental starting point.

The public transport provision theme includes a number of problems begging for solutions, but first it is necessary to understand the causes of these problems. The drawing of a diagram to explore causes of success in public transport provision is extremely difficult. You could well accept this as a challenge to practise causal diagramming in a difficult area. There are problems of under-funding, poor provision, lack of reliability, poor image or poor integration with other forms of transport. A series of Multiple-Cause diagrams based upon each of these problems could be linked together to provide a more holistic view of the situation. When looking at the influences on public transport provision (see Figure 5.13), road congestion influence leads to a perceived need, yet one problem is of low demand in many places. The causes of declining demand can be a useful area to diagram.

When using the diagram in Figure 7.4 as a means of thinking through the problem of declining demand it is important that the link between each set of components can be defended as being causal in some way. The diagrammer should be able to point to each link and say, 'This is a necessary cause', or 'a sufficient cause', or 'a contributory cause'. A necessary cause can be seen between increasing car use and increasing road congestion; if car use (A) decreased then road congestion (B) would also decrease. The two are tied by a necessary bond. That something is a necessary cause does not preclude other causes too, such as heavy vehicle use in this case. However, the evidence for being a necessary cause is very strong here. A strong contender for a sufficient cause is the link between increased cost to the user (A) and a decline in demand (B). That occurrence A leads to B is highly possible, but B can occur without this particular A. The component of poor integration with other transport use could be seen as a contributory cause. The non-existence of integration may have little causal influence on declining demand, but again the diagram is making us think through this possi-

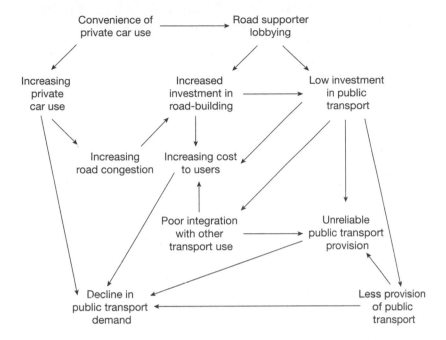

Figure 7.4   Multiple-Cause diagram of declining demand
for public transport

bility. There are four sufficient causes, on this evidence, of declining demand: an increase in car use, increased cost to users, poor reliability and less provision. The diagram demonstrates how these causes are linked together so that no single cause of this problem exists.

In summary, to describe something as being the cause of something else requires a good deal of thought and an appreciation that different kinds of cause exist.

Sometimes you will come across 'cause effect' diagrams, but 'effect' is a poor word to describe the outcome of a multiple-cause situation. Outcomes of this nature normally have rather more impact than simply being an 'effect', and this applies whether we are exploring causes of problems or causes of success. Normally we are seeking to explain the causal influences behind catastrophe, failure, collapse or disaster on the one hand, or behind success, innovation, pleasure or creativeness on the other. This amounts to rather more than simply 'effect'.

BUSINESS PURPOSES OF THE MULTIPLE-CAUSE DIAGRAM

• Use the Multiple-Cause diagram whenever it is necessary to locate cause or, more likely, causes of a problem. This can be done in advance of an activity, to help anticipate causes occurring, or in retrospect to explain why a problem happened.

- Use this diagram when others appear to have difficulty in separating symptoms from causes, or when the very concept of causation appears to be poorly understood.
- The Multiple-Cause diagram is invaluable in helping to explain reasons for a particular failure, whether of a machine, a process, team-working or an adopted policy.

SUMMARY AND CONVENTIONS

In summary, whenever Multiple-Cause diagrams are read it is necessary to take account of the kinds of cause, whether necessary, sufficient or simply contributory. When drawing this diagram the end result is almost inevitably a network or spider-web like pattern. Be very suspicious of any linear-type pattern that is more likely to indicate a flow relationship of some kind. It is reasonable to say that the concept of cause is poorly understood. If Aristotle suddenly appeared today he would be quite surprised that all his work on this subject has not yet been fully adopted. No doubt it will take time.

Conventions for the Multiple-Cause diagram

- All statements must be actions.
- People or objects alone cannot be causal.
- There needs to be an end point or termination to this diagram that shows clearly what is being caused.
- Arrows are used only one way to show direction from cause (A) to action being caused (B).
- Multiple causes rarely occur in a straight linear way: there are normally interactions that lead to a 'web-like' pattern.
- The title must give the type of diagram and the subject being caused.

Fishbone diagram

The diagram is given this name because it looks like a fishbone, complete with head (see Figure 7.5).

This Fishbone, known also by the originator name as Ishikawa diagram, is closely related to the Multiple-Cause diagram. The main difference is that here we look at a specific problem, recognize the main

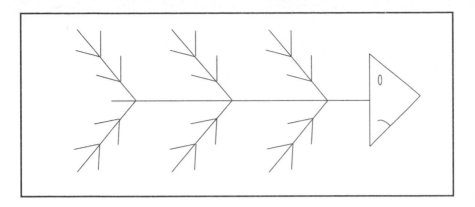

Figure 7.5 Fishbone diagram (outline)

areas of fault that can lead to this problem, and for each area of fault identify the possible causes. Information of this kind could be provided in a list, but listing would miss some crucial interactions between faults and causes. The fishbone gives us greater insight into the dynamics of the situation. The key problem is placed inside the head of the fish, then an area of fault is put against each larger bone. When this has been done, the result may be a small, large or very large fish. The smaller bones are used to show the possible causes that can be associated with a fault area. It is important to appreciate that the separating of main bones in the diagram does not mean a necessary separating of fault areas. One aim is to recognize where common causes exist across the whole diagram, and then explore what interaction could exist between these causes. A Multiple-Cause diagram is probably the best tool for this next stage. When used in this way, two diagrams can complement each other.

BUSINESS APPLICATION OF THE FISHBONE DIAGRAM

A completed Fishbone diagram, to illustrate a problem not uncommon in business, is given in Figure 7.6. The larger bones can be labelled from A to however many bones are shown to indicate some key feature about the broad problem areas. Bone A could be the fault-area that shows up most often whenever the problem exists. For example, whenever the problem as stated at the head is experienced, eight times out of ten the area of fault shown at bone A will be involved. The bone marked as B would be next in order of frequency, and so on. Alternatively, bone A could be the area of fault that has the most serious impact on the problem, and other bones are then labelled in order of estimated impact.

The smaller bones, showing possible causes, are numbered from 1 in priority order, and again the order can be based on frequency of occurrence, estimated impact or any other criteria used for prioritizing.

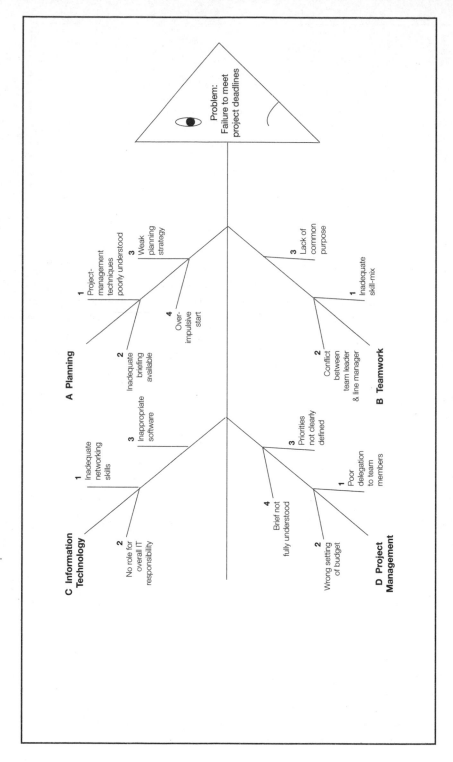

Figure 7.6 Fishbone diagram of failure to meet project deadlines

For any problem, what we can recognize as a possible area of fault is stated in the head. This area is sometimes referred to as the 'problem space' because it is the area where a solution to the problem is most likely to exist. Planning is seen as critical in Figure 7.6. What is the main fault to be identified here? How many causes can be identified? The overall aim is to reduce this area as quickly as possible to a size where the solution can be identified. For each possible fault there is normally more than one cause, and among these causes there can be at times a root or ultimate cause. When causes have been identified it is possible to check back to faults. For example, 'What main fault occurs as a result of project-management techniques being poorly understood?' Put another way, 'What is the main consequence of having this cause?' When this cause exists, what fault or faults occur in project work?

The Fishbone diagram may be drawn with no particular order given to the large or smaller bones; in this case what you see in the diagram is interpreted by asking questions about all the fault-areas and causes displayed. The outcome could be that two areas of faults are especially critical and share common causes which, in turn, makes these causes ripe for attention.

Every problem has normally one or more associated faults, errors, discrepancies or whatever label you wish to use. A fault is the 'thing' that must be fixed in order to remove the problem. Confusion can arise when people treat a fault as though it must automatically be the cause of a problem. Each fault has a cause, or more than one cause. Treating the fault and not the cause or causes normally leads to frequent repetition of the problem.

A Fishbone diagram could be used to summarize the process of medical diagnosis. Going to see a medical doctor with a persistent pain (symptom) is to address a problem, that could be put in the head of the fish. The doctor looks for signs that will lead to a location of possible faults. When the fault has been located, there needs to be an explanation by exploring possible causes with the aim of identifying a root cause.

It is not uncommon for a technician only to repair faults, while ignoring causes, and to go on repairing the same faults. In the area of crime, shoplifting is 'fixed' by fining or imprisonment. Shoplifting is seen as a cause of lost profit, so mistakenly it is seen as a cause rather than, in reality, a fault which in turn has a number of possible causes, largely ignored. As with the technician and experience of repetitive faults, the shoplifting faults seldom reduce in number. There is a link with the closed-loop Control diagram here. Fixing only faults is an example of continually going around the closed loop in response to problems at the sensor. In contrast, the attention given to causes leads automatically to activities at the input, or the fundamental basis of a process.

The Fishbone is an ideal diagram for group work, where people can be involved in agreeing on the problem to be placed at the head, and in the building up of individual bones.

When causes have been located and remedial action taken, the Fishbone can be revisited and drawn again to reflect the changes. The new diagram may, but hopefully will not, show that another fault area has been created or that other causes have emerged.

BUSINESS PURPOSE OF THE FISHBONE DIAGRAM

- One of the main purposes of the Fishbone diagram in business is to capture, in one picture, all aspects of a particular problem. Most commonly this is used in engineering settings, whether in a large chemical plant or among service engineers looking after City Information Technology (IT) equipment. Major recurring problems can often be dealt with in a reactive way by busy people simply wanting to get a system back to full performance, but in the long term this practice is normally very inefficient. There needs to be time for analysis of recurring problems, their faults and especially causes. The Multiple-Case and Fishbone diagrams in tandem are ideal tools for this purpose.
- Look upon the Fishbone diagram as a logical extension of the Multiple-Cause diagram. Key themes can be extracted from a Multiple-Cause diagram to be developed as main bones, then causes associated with each theme can be plotted as smaller bones.
- The Fishbone provides a more structured pattern than is possible with the Multiple-Cause approach, and it is easier to recognize relationships between causes. On the other hand the Fishbone does lack the holist view and real dynamics provided by the Multiple-Cause. Use both types of diagram and benefit from the richness of each one.

SUMMARY AND CONVENTIONS

In summary, the Fishbone diagram provides a good example of seeing a problem in terms of causes with the added advantage of clear structure. The diagram enables us to see fault areas and related causes in one picture of possible linkages. A non-holistic alternative is to look for the simple expedient of finding someone to blame for a problem, or seeing faults and related causes only in a simple linear way.

Conventions for the fishbone diagram

- Define the problem clearly first and place in the head.

- Brainstorm or brain-write areas of faults/errors associated with the problem and allocate one larger bone to each.
- Use the smaller bones to show causes associated with the particular area of faults.
- Avoid the confusion between faults and causes.
- Make sure the problem at the head has been clearly defined and is not simply a symptom of the problem – again the drawing of the diagram makes you think about this issue.
- Look for common causes across the diagram.

Sign diagram

The Sign diagram can add further useful information to the idea of causation by indicating the direction that the cause is taking. By adding the signs of + (plus) or – (minus) the direction of causal influence can be effectively read as an account of what is happening directly from the diagram. The extract from a Multiple-Cause diagram in Figure 7.7 can be 'read' in two ways:

1. *If* cigarette smoking increases *then* confined-space air pollution also increases.
2. *If* cigarette smoking decreases *then* confined-space air pollution also decreases.

The same reading is made to general pollution and to passive smoking. This is an example of positive feedback covered in Chapter 4, on control. Whatever happens at A will be copied in B, or, put another way, B is reinforcing A. This means that there is no negative control loop to help maintain a required standard and equilibrium. For every percentage *increase* in A, there should be a similar *increase* in B, C and D – as long as

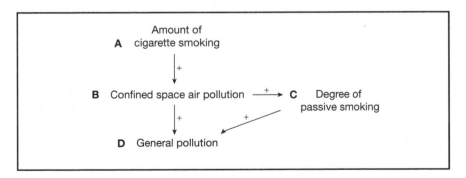

Figure 7.7 Sign diagram (extract from lung cancer causation)

there is a positive sign in place. Also, for every percentage *decrease* in A there should be a similar *decrease* in B, C and D – as long as a positive sign is in place.

This is where some people have difficulty with this particular diagram: positive, as in positive correlation between two events, means that as one (A) goes up the other (B) goes up too, and as one (A) goes down the other (B) goes down too.

An important point to note when drawing a Sign diagram is that you never put values on the statements. The event is simply stated as 'cigarette smoking', and <u>not</u> as *more* or *less* cigarette smoking. The diagram must be 'read' as either more of or less of something or as either increase in or decrease in something. If you put a value in the diagram statements then reading can sound like, 'more of less cigarette smoking', which is unnecessary confusion and is to be avoided.

Room heating provides an everyday example of cause and direction of cause to provide control (Figure 7.8). The causal link between outside temperature and room temperature cannot be included within the loop because it is not possible to influence or control the climate, which is a root cause of temperature fluctuation. Now go around the sign graph, starting at any point, and 'read' what it is telling you, as explained in the discussion of Figure 7.7. In reality a central-heating system operates around such a loop to maintain a comfortable range of temperature. The heating-control process is compensating for the fact that we cannot control outside temperature.

BUSINESS APPLICATION OF THE SIGN DIAGRAM

The Sign diagram could be used to summarize the relationship between customers and sales and could look like this:

This reads as: 'An *increase* in number of customers leads to an *increase* in the amount of sales', or as: 'A *decrease* in the number of customers leads to a *decrease* in the amount of sales'.

The – (minus) sign when used reflects negative feedback and again is 'read' in two ways:

1. *If* A goes up *then* B goes down.
2. *If* A goes down *then* B goes up.

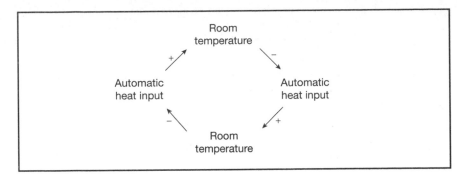

Figure 7.8 Sign diagram of room temperature control

One way to make this relationship real is to stand with arms outstretched sideways: for plus (+) relationship one arm (A) goes up as the other arm (B) also goes up in the air, and as (A) goes down by your side the other arm (B) goes down to your side, in unison. For minus (−) relationship, if one arm (A) goes up in the air, the other arm (B) goes down to your side, in unison, and as (A) goes down to your side, arm (B) goes up into the air. The relationship between price and sales could look like this:

PRICE   SALES

This is read as: 'Increased price leads to lower sales', or as: 'Decreased price leads to higher sales'. While this causal relationship is not true at all times, it is far more realistic than putting a plus sign between price and sales, though even here sellers of 'image' products to highly gullible customers would see sense in a plus sign. In such a case the price may well keep on rising because it is being reinforced by positive feedback.

A complete Sign diagram will illustrate how plus and minus signs are combined to illustrate in a rather simplified way a common dilemma shown in Figure 7.9. The diagram can be read as: 'If rate of income tax is *increased*, disposable income will *decrease* (−); then sale of goods will also *decrease* (+) and tax revenue from these sales will also *decrease* (+); then the need for more tax revenue will *increase* (−), and taxation will increase (+).'

The diagram can also be read as: 'If rate of income tax is *decreased*, the disposable income of people will *increase* (−); then sale of goods will also *increase* (+) and tax revenue from sales will also *increase* (+); then the need for tax revenue decreases (−) and taxation can also be *decreased* (+).'

The even number of minus signs in the diagram has a positive effect, so it is still working as positive feedback: whatever happens in direction, whether up or down, will be reinforced and cause either further increase or further decrease. When there is an odd number of minus signs in a

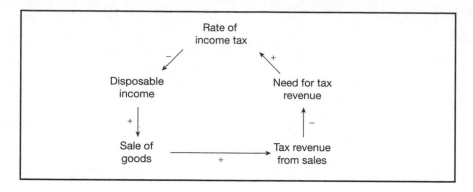

Figure 7.9   Sign diagram (simplified) of taxation and sales

diagram there is more likely to be stability or at least an oscillation around a required state.

When John Maynard Keynes, the economist, produced his basic model of incomes, production and consumption he was not aware of the Sign diagram. In Figure 7.10 his model is presented in this way. In practice the model shows positive feedback rather than equilibrium. The immediate thing to be noted from looking at the arrows is that 'rate of investment' is the only independent part of the diagram; all other parts are dependent on each other. Where there is a closed loop of interdependence, as shown in this diagram, with positive reinforcing causes, the outcome is very often instability. Only one element needs to change significantly for any hope of equilibrium to be upset.

When Sign diagrams are used to help analyse a complex situation such as the economy, use of public transport or the control of futures dealing, the aim is to identify points of intervention where the cycle can be broken and any problem removed. The intervention points in the room-temperature example are simply at the heat inputs, which can be controlled automatically or adjusted manually. More complex situations,

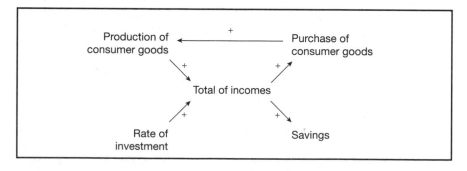

Figure 7.10   Sign diagram of Keynes' model for equilibrium

involving people, need rather more thought. The Sign diagram can suddenly show where key issues exist, and where action needs to be taken. One intervention point in the taxation and sales dilemma appears to be a transfer from the direct taxation, releasing more disposable income, to the indirect tax from sales revenue. The task of producing such a diagram also encourages different ways of thinking about a well-known problem. The original passive smoking example used in a much earlier Multiple-Cause diagram (Figure 7.1) simply showed a link from cigarette smoking to passive smoking. When signs were added, it was realized that the statement of, 'more smoking leads to more passive smoking (+)' is not strictly true; it is unlikely that smoking hill-walkers would pose the threat of passive smoking. There is an intervening issue of confined-space pollution and it is the increase or decrease in this that influences passive smoking. The original Multiple-Cause diagram was then changed to show this added issue.

Some readers are likely to disagree with some or even all of this analysis, but one way to clarify the differences and promote rational discussion is to have conflicting diagrams available for comparison.

The increase in private car use is a factor in the debate about public transport use, so it can be analysed by using a Sign diagram, and this provides yet another perspective on this theme (Figure 7.11). Now 'read' this rather more complex diagram, starting at any point with the words, 'an increase in leads to . . .' or as 'a decrease in leads to . . .', taking account of the signs on the arrows. With scrap paper and a pencil you could draw your own Sign diagram perception of this problem, that could well be very different. The perspective shown here indicates 'road building' as an intervention point for action.

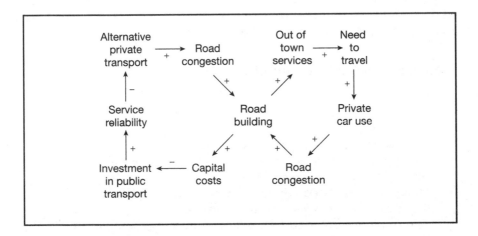

Figure 7.11 Sign diagram of private car use

BUSINESS PURPOSE OF THE SIGN DIAGRAM

- When seeking to increase sales of goods or a service it is helpful to know about the particular activities that promote positive feedback. How do we ensure that effective actions become reinforced so that they go on increasing their effectiveness, thereby increasing the chances of yet higher performance? Drawing a Sign diagram of key components allows us to see the positive feedback at work. Remember too that we can also see positive feedback of *ineffective* actions leading to yet further decrease in performance.
- When we wish to control an activity or a process so that stability is maintained, such as a particular quality standard for manufactured goods, or a standard of service, then we can look to negative feedback. There are times when the cost of quality is too high when compared with the price being charged for goods or service; a consistent level of appropriate quality is required and the correcting actions from negative feedback meet this need.

SUMMARY AND CONVENTIONS

In summary, the inclusion of signs adds a useful dimension to the way we think about the action of one thing upon another. Do we decrease the amount of cigarette advertising in an attempt to decrease the amount of cigarette smoking (+)? Or do we increase the amount of warnings about a possible danger to health in an attempt to decrease the amount of cigarette smoking (–)? Decisions we must make from time to time often include positive or negative feedback of this kind; the Sign diagram helps focus attention on this part of decision-making. One of the most important uses of the Sign diagram is to reach a stage where an intervention point can be recognized, so that we can break into the cycle and make a change that can improve the situation.

Conventions for the Sign diagram

- Statements must be free of any values such as 'more', 'less', 'increase' or 'decrease'.
- Statements need to be actions of some kind.
- Plus signs are used where an increase or decrease in A leads to a similar increase or decrease in B.
- Minus signs are used where an increase in A leads to a decrease in B, or a decrease in A leads to an increase in B.
- Sign diagrams are read by starting with 'an increase in this leads to . . .', or as 'a decrease in this leads to . . .'.

8 Diagramming for change

Force-field diagram

The originator of this diagram was psychologist Kurt Lewin (pronounced 'le-veen'), who died in 1947. He developed a number of diagrams, similar to the Influence type, to illustrate how forces of various kinds can help explain aspects of human behaviour. The Force-Field diagram has proved to be of enormous benefit to industries faced with major change. The diagram remains powerful as a tool to be used in any form of change where people are actively involved. It is also very useful when making a decision about the introduction of a new product or service. Here the aim is to highlight valid reasons for the introduction and to be alerted to possible restraining forces, some of which if not taken into account could lead to the failure of a planned venture or innovation.

Whenever change is planned there are normally one or more individuals who are committed to the plan, and who have what they see as valid reasons for moving away from the established way of doing things. In Lewin's terms these reasons can be seen as driving forces. People who question the change, or who are totally opposed to it, will give reasons for either serious questioning or outright opposition. These reasons can be seen as restraining forces.

The idea of forces, applied in this way, is shown by the diagram outline in Figure 8.1. The arrows, showing forces, are drawn in different thicknesses to indicate perceived strength of force in each case. (Alternatively, the arrows can be drawn at different lengths.) The central box must contain a clear concise statement of what is being proposed. When change of any kind is managed effectively, the first step is to state the change and reasons (driving forces) and gather responses from those involved. From these responses it is sometimes possible to add further to the number of driving forces, but also include in the diagram any restraining forces, or 'downside' of the proposal.

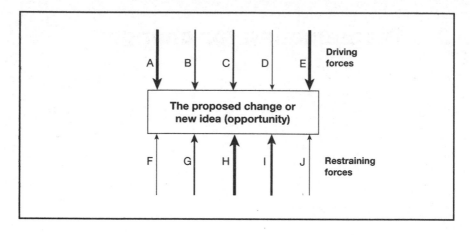

Figure 8.1   Force-Field diagram (outline)

Business application of the force-field diagram

The diagram can be used for change management, new product development, new career/job evaluation or whenever forces can be seen as acting upon choice.

A practical example of the Force-Field diagram in use is based on the change from traditional newspaper printing methods to accommodate the development of new technology. In this case, practices that had witnessed steady evolutionary changes over three hundred years were suddenly the subject of revolutionary change. A Force-Field diagram can capture some of the main driving and restraining forces as these were perceived to exist at the time of the change. In business terms, there were a number of persuasive reasons why such change ought to take place. Some of the reasons were stronger than others and this is shown, in an estimated way, by thickness of arrow. In more personal terms, there were strong reasons for not making the change, and again different strengths are illustrated in the same way. A common feature of changes in organizations is that reasons for change are often valid in business terms, while the reasons given as restraining forces are often more personal in nature.

The diagram allows us to see, at a glance, the dynamics of a proposed change. As a result of seeing Figure 8.2, people in the industry could be expected to add further forces. Unfortunately, the picture we see leads frequently to a two-sided view of the situation or a 'them' and 'us' outcome. Taking a holist view by considering the different forces together, rather than as two separate issues, goes a long way to managing a change more effectively. The Force-Field diagram helps us to recognize that the same reason can exist on both sides. The decrease in union power can be seen as a reason for change and as such is a driver,

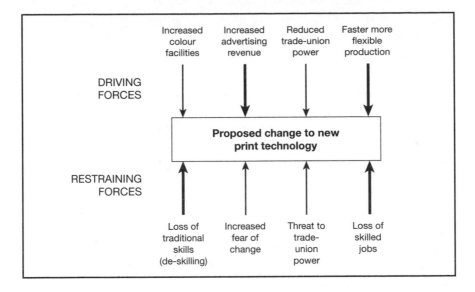

Figure 8.2   Force-Field diagram of change to new print technology

but the associated threat to this power can also be seen as a reason for resisting the change and becomes a restraining force, depending upon our perception of the situation.

It is possible to redraw the Force-Field diagram to show the reasons for not changing as being the driving forces, and this simple reversal does put a different perspective on the proposed change.

Another issue raised by this diagram is the persuasiveness of certain words. The idea of 'driving' can easily be seen as positive and therefore as somehow 'good' or certainly better than the rather negative sound of 'restraining'. In any change people may use 'modern' or 'modernize' in a similar way when there is no valid reason for assuming that 'modern' or 'modernize' are automatically better, or to be preferred to a word such as 'traditional', or vice versa. There is a danger that the persuasive force of the words blinds people to the real issues involved in the change. The diagram simply alerts everyone involved to the critical reasons for adopting one stance or the other. In practice, the outcome from this diagram can be treated in, at least, five ways.

1   Ignore the restraining forces and concentrate only on the drivers, to make the change happen.
2   Take account of the restraining forces, and increase the power of selected drivers to make the change happen.
3   Take account of restraining forces and take action to remove people's objections.

4   Increase force of drivers and decrease the force of restrainers tog-
     ether.
5   Take account of restraining forces and abandon the idea.

The first two options in the list normally leads to more difficulties later,
because the reasons given as restraining forces rarely go away. The third
and fourth options involve more time and effort that may or may not be
repaid by having fewer difficulties later. The fifth option, an example
being the change that introduced the UK poll tax, can save much time
and effort if done sufficiently early.

     The actual wording of the forces needs care. To be a force there must
be an action – the description needs to be of something being done. The
same point has been made for the Influence and Multiple-Cause
diagrams. A person such as 'manager' or 'doctor' cannot be a force; only
by doing something can force be exerted. There must be some plausible
reason, for driving or restraining, that has been well thought out and
can be defended. The box in the centre of the diagram contains the
subject that has generated these forces. It is common for the subject to be
one of proposed change, but it can be any proposed activity such as the
introduction of a new product, or a possible new career. 'This new job
I'm thinking of taking, what are the drivers and what are the restrainers?' Note that these forces are different from considering advantages or
disadvantages of a new job, which is a more common way of making
such a choice. A new job advantage could be 'pleasant environment' but
this is not a force; nothing is happening to make it a force, but it is
typical of an advantage. The force being described is not necessarily a
cause either. A force can be making something happen but cannot be a
cause because it has not yet happened. It is important to appreciate the
nature of force in this way.

     It is interesting to think of how the Force-Field diagram can be used
before the introduction of a new product. The example given here is of
a new idea for holding papers together temporarily as an advance on
the conventional paper-clip. The result has been a dispenser that
delivers flat steel clips. Someone had to think of this incremental
change to an existing product, and then persuade someone to market
and manufacture the finished item. For any innovation of this kind, a
point is reached where 'for' and 'against' factors need to be considered.
The Force-Field diagram is ideal for this purpose, but conceptually the
idea of 'force' carries more meaning than simply being for or against, or
having advantages and disadvantages associated with the proposed
product. Typical forces that could be considered in this case are shown
in Figure 8.3.

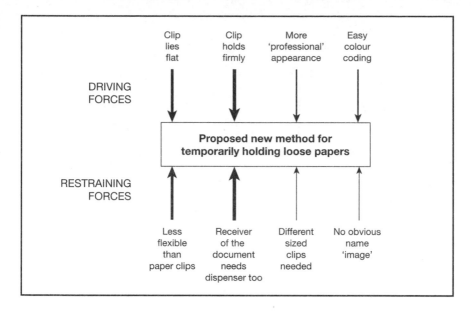

Figure 8.3 Force-Field diagram of new product idea

On balance the diagram indicates a good chance of success if users can see the driving forces outweighing the restraining forces. The restraining force of 'document receiver needing a dispenser', if they wish to remove papers and then put them back again with the clip, could be seen as a driving force in marketing terms – more dispensers will need to be sold. The diagram was done in hindsight because the idea has now been transformed into a very effective way to hold papers. The perceived restraining forces still exist, but appear to be outweighed by the driving forces.

Force-Field diagrams can be used to explore a number of issues related to public transport provision, and most of these will be concerned with proposed changes of some kind. One of these changes could be a transfer of direct taxation on vehicles to an additional indirect tax on the cost of fuel – see Figure 8.4. Without any conscious effort to make it happen, the driving forces are related to wide government-type issues while the restraining forces are business-focused. If such a change were to take place it would be necessary to address the restraining forces, at the same time addressing other restraining forces that could come from a wider consultation exercise.

BUSINESS PURPOSE OF THE FORCE-FIELD DIAGRAM

- The convention for showing the direction of forces has been inwards

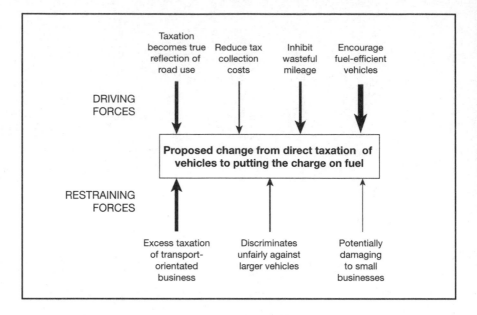

Figure 8.4   Force-Field diagram of proposed
change in vehicle taxation

towards the subject, as shown by the diagrams drawn here: to make it happen or to make it not happen. Sometimes both sets of arrows are shown going away from the subject box so there is a pull in one direction, and an opposing pull, like a tug-of-war. Both ways, inwards or outwards, are acceptable and convey the essential idea of opposing forces. Showing both sets of arrows in the same direction must be avoided. In the idea of pulling or pushing there is a possible metaphor for how the respective 'sides' treat the situation, as pulling in opposite directions or as confrontational. The metaphor is worth holding in mind when next faced with conflict over a proposed change.

- The initial statement written in the box needs a good deal of thought; as pointed out in the drawing of the Input-Output diagram, this 'boxed' statement is not necessarily as obvious as it may seem. The purpose implied by this statement largely dictates the forces to be drawn. The diagram serves a useful purpose in this respect by imposing a discipline to think clearly and concisely about the proposed change or proposed new idea. There are examples in the newspaper industry of change to new technology being forced through without taking any account of restraining forces, and rioting was the outcome. The reader ought to be able to reflect on other change, such as an introduction of poll taxing, where only the driving forces had been considered and action taken without adequate thinking about the full implications. Within organizations, quite small changes such as swapping offices can have an adverse impact if restraining forces are overlooked. The Force-Field diagram has provided an extremely useful tool in the management of change and for the innovation and marketing of new products.

SUMMARY AND CONVENTIONS

In summary, the Force-Field diagram has a number of uses, but probably its widest application is in the area of change management. There are applications also in the development of new products, or for helping people decide upon important moves in their lives. The diagram is equally powerful in these areas, so the diagram's wider use ought to be encouraged.

Conventions for the Force-Field diagram

- State the subject clearly inside the horizontal box, typically a proposed change, a new product or a new type of service.
- Show the driving and restraining forces as thicker/thinner according to estimated strength of the force.
- Always show both sets of arrows as being in opposite directions, either as opposing forces, head on, or as pulling in opposite directions.
- State each force clearly as action that is capable of being a force, and can be defended as such.
- Label driving forces and restraining forces on the diagram to show clearly the perception being taken.

The Window diagram

First reference was made to the Window diagram as Johari's Window showing a simple four-pane design, which over the years has developed numerous uses; in fact anything that can be shown as two-by-two options will fit into the basic Window diagram. Unlike the Force-Field diagram, in the last section, choice is seen as going beyond two opposing forces and can be represented by an array of choices in matrix form.

The Window diagram in practice is often of the four-pane model, but can have a number of panes, as shown in Figure 8.5. One of the early uses of the Window diagram was in the demonstration of logic reasoning through the use of syllogisms. The well-known writer Charles Dodgson (Lewis Carroll) published a book in 1887 entitled *The Game of*

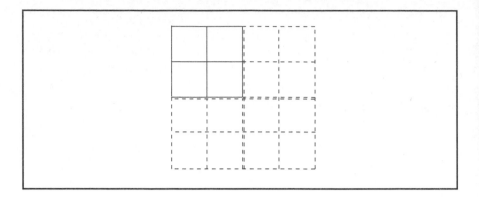

Figure 8.5   Window diagram (outline)

Logic. The book included an envelope to hold the diagram and nine coloured counters. The diagram was of two four-pane windows, one set inside the other. The counters were moved about the diagram depending upon how the syllogism was being used, the premises separately or combined, and the conclusion.

Business application of the Window diagram

One of the best known applications of the window is the SWOT diagram (Figure 8.6). The SWOT diagram has a very wide range of uses such as personal development, design of widgets or analysis of organizations.

The Window diagram, like all diagrams, relies heavily upon the perception of the person who does the drawing. This needs repeating because it can be easy to see strengths, weaknesses, opportunities and threats as somehow absolute in any one situation.

The SWOT diagram can be applied to any situation where people come together whether at work, in families, clubs or sporting teams. At the individual level, the diagram can be a very useful tool in the choice of job or career. A personal SWOT can be done that covers all four parts of the diagram in as much detail as possible. The next step is to attempt a reversal exercise, to see how far the weaknesses may be viewed alternatively as strengths, and the threats as possible opportunities. When this has been done, the revised diagram is reconsidered to ask questions about strengths and opportunities. Which job or career offers the best prospects of fully exploiting the stated strengths? What opportunities can be developed further? This positive line of thinking needs to be pushed as far as possible until some realistic and even not so realistic career options have been generated. From these options at least one firm decision can hopefully be made. The weaknesses and threats that still exist after the

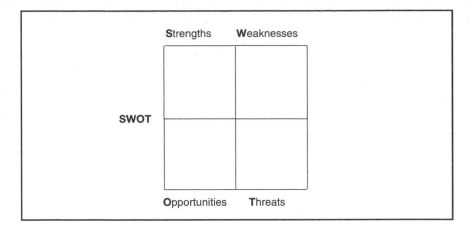

Figure 8.6   SWOT diagram (outline)

reversal exercise are then thought about in the light of the final decision. It may still be possible to see particular weaknesses as strengths, or threats as opportunities. Where this is not possible, the next step is to decide what can be done about threats and weaknesses that would clearly have an influence upon any option being followed. A diagram of this kind can provide a structured framework that allows you to focus on key issues while at the same time presenting an overall picture.

Strengths, weaknesses, opportunities and threats could be recorded as four lists down or across a page, but the boxing provided by the diagram does serve an important role. The space within a box represents an area, and when a threat has been recognized alternatively as an opportunity it actually transfers into an area of opportunity that may well contain other opportunities. The bounding of the area is important too because we are made to consider any special features about the contents in one box before crossing a boundary to concentrate upon other features. For example, someone may discover that nearly all opportunities are highly individualized, while most threats involve other people, or vice versa. Or again, find that nearly all strengths are business and financially orientated while most weaknesses involve some kind of relationship issue, or vice versa. This kind of food for thought can come quite easily as the eye ranges from one boxed area to another in this way.

There is nothing absolute about any one of these categories; one can be seen as the other if necessary. At times of uncertain employment prospects some people may write 'fear of redundancy' as a threat when asked to think about their current job. When the idea of reversal is used to convert threats, the fear of redundancy can be seen equally well as an opportunity arising from redundancy and can be re-written as, 'added scope offered by redundancy' and moved across from threats box to the opportunity box. The act of viewing a situation differently in this way can lead to a different perspective on change. Another example is when someone, asked to think of their own characteristics, writes 'quiet' as a weakness. This too could be reversed by re-writing as 'quiet effective listener' and moved to a strength. The description of 'competitive' may often be written as a strength but can equally be seen as a weakness, depending upon the circumstances.

There is an ongoing interplay between these four features of the SWOT diagram. Sometimes it is not necessary, nor desirable, to reverse the contents of the boxes in this way. The descriptions can be accepted as being what they are, and appropriate actions taken. A total acceptance of SWOT is more likely to occur when designing new objects or schemes where certain features have to be accepted. When contemplating a new shopping complex for example, a number of SWOT diagrams can be done on suitable location, planning, layout, type of design, or transport access. For each of these subjects, the weakness and threats need to be known and addressed individually as part of an early process of exploration and feasibility. The strengths and opportunities need to be known in the same way so that ideas can be generated to exploit them still further. Even here, the chance to see weaknesses as possible strengths and threats as opportunities should not be overlooked. The same is true when we think of how organizations, or departments within organizations, perform.

The use of a SWOT diagram can be particularly helpful for groups of people working together but not in close proximity, such as in a sales team with members working in different locations (see Figure 8.7), or a field maintenance team of engineers who travel a good deal. In these circumstances, each person could produce a SWOT diagram quite independently on their perception of the team's work, then diagrams are brought together, either when a convenient meeting allows or by computer networking.

An exercise of this kind can highlight critical issues, and much can be learned from an exploration of the results. Looking at the 'weaknesses' part of the window, the business may simply have to act on networking as a problem. Inadequate training may not be the same as inadequate learning; what strengths are available to facilitate learning as opposed to thinking only about training? Competition between sales teams could be seen as a strength if a more autonomous profit-centred approach could be adopted. Can too little personal contact be seen instead as greater scope for personal initiative?

The SWOT diagram is not confined to individual or team use: there are wider organizational issues that can be examined by making use of the diagram. An example, not uncommon at the present time, is for certain organizations to move from wholly funded, not-for-profit operation to a

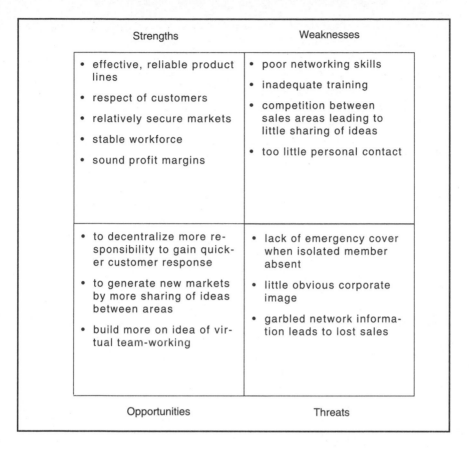

Strengths	Weaknesses
• effective, reliable product lines • respect of customers • relatively secure markets • stable workforce • sound profit margins	• poor networking skills • inadequate training • competition between sales areas leading to little sharing of ideas • too little personal contact
• to decentralize more re-sponsibility to gain quick-er customer response • to generate new markets by more sharing of ideas between areas • build more on idea of vir-tual team-working	• lack of emergency cover when isolated member absent • little obvious corporate image • garbled network informa-tion leads to lost sales
Opportunities	Threats

Figure 8.7 SWOT diagram of sales team working remotely

more commercial profit-centred way of working. A planned change of this kind can be presented as a Force-Field diagram, showing drivers of the change together with restraining forces. Then a SWOT diagram builds upon this picture by making people who advocate the change face up to possible weaknesses and threats. Similarly those who generate the restraining forces can see possible strengths and opportunities.

A further development of this approach is to have a SWOT diagram drawn to show the strengths, weaknesses, opportunities and threats of the business before the planned change. When this has been done a second diagram can be drawn, this time showing the SWOT features as they ought to exist after the change. A SWOT exercise as part of such a transition can be very helpful in pointing to critical areas that need atten-tion. Or someone may draw a diagram and see new opportunities, although they began by seeing only threats from the planned change. Another view from the diagram may show a need to build on existing strengths that are applicable to the new ways of working, or the need to take action over present weaknesses.

It should not be too difficult to recognize a strong link between SWOT and the Force-Field diagram considered in the previous section. When seeking to introduce change, people will quickly point to opportunities as driving forces, and to the strengths that allow the opportunities to be exploited. People who are ready to question or oppose change will readily point to threats, possible threats and to weaknesses that can make change too risky. The contents of a Force-Field diagram can often be reflected in the contents of a SWOT diagram if done within the same group or overall business. However, the diagrams do have different purposes. The Force-Field diagram is used to help satisfy a specific objective: to make change X or not, or to market product Y or not. In contrast the SWOT diagram is more exploratory, and can be used to examine critical features of a person, group or product, and to promote further discussion which in turn should lead to better-informed decisions. The two diagrams are linked and can be used in a comple-mentary way. The SWOT diagram is useful when trying to resolve issues suggested by the restraining forces in a Force-Field diagram. If, for example, restraining forces are typically given as 'lack of skills', 'inadequate finance', 'uncertainty', 'becoming too big' or 'loss of status', a SWOT diagram completed independently by people who contribute to the restraining forces would help them elaborate on their views. There is an added advantage that people who oppose a particular change can show, through the diagram, what they see as strengths and opportuni-ties from the act of not changing. The entries provide a different perspective from those who are promoting the change. If this wider view is not allowed, then people in opposition to change are seen only in a negative light as saying 'no' to what is being called 'progress' or 'modernization'. The same approach, with the SWOT diagram, can be used to allow for supporters of the driving forces to elaborate on their views. The end result is a much broader picture embracing wider views that should encourage informed debate.

There are, like the SWOT diagram, other well-known uses of the Window. In Figure 8.8 there is a comparison between two types of management style and two types of employee style. The way to use this diagram is to write descriptions of typical examples in the boxes. What example of behaviour can you think of from experience that best fits into box B? This would be an example of styles not matching. An autocratic manager can only function effectively when most employees are happy to be obedient. Introducing people with an independent style can be expected to cause problems, and is the subject of box B.

There is much reference to management style in the literature but

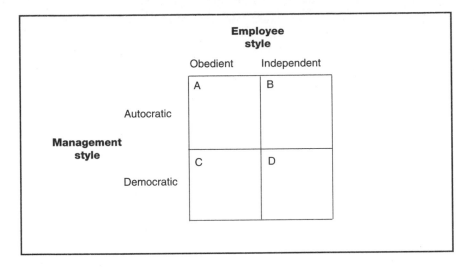

Figure 8.8 Window diagram of management/employee styles

little thought given to employee style and how the respective styles either match or do not match. A 2 by 2 Window diagram captures a picture of these relationships very well. We can see at a glance that the autocratic style can only really function in Box A, and the democratic style in Box D, and that non-matching styles, Boxes B and C, are likely to cause problems. Readers of the diagram should be able to think of situations where interpersonal issues arise because of the conflict of styles to be found in Box B or Box C. Where most management–employee activity is perceived to fall into the areas of these two boxes warning bells ought to be ringing.

The Window can be extended to take account of other categories of management style and employee style. By using a 4 by 4 window, the styles autocratic, democratic, parental and collegiate can be written down one side as management styles, and employee styles can be shown along the top as obedient, independent, dependent and autonomous. Now, sixteen boxes can be examined for typical examples of either match or mismatch of styles.

You may like to draw such a diagram, ponder on which panes are most relevant to him or her, and think about what could be written in these parts of the Window.

Another simple, but effective, use of the Window is to show how information can be handled within a group of people. There are situations where a particular item of information or level of awareness, relevant to others, is known to one person in a group but is not known by any other person in the group. A common term for a situation of this kind is to call it a hidden agenda (see box B in Figure 8.9). A reverse situation is when all group members, apart from one, know of information or have appropriate awareness (see box C). Here the one person is often described as having a blind spot. A term like 'group cohesion' or 'cognisance' could be given to box A in the diagram, but it equally can be viewed using the term 'group-think'. The reader can ascribe a term to box D. Again, descriptions of typical examples of behaviour from group-working can be written in the boxes.

When a Window diagram is extended to include more than four panes the result is often referred to as a story-board. When pictures are used instead of words the diagram can be known by the term cartoon story-board.

One useful way to use diagrams as a means of thinking through a problem is to capture a progressive story from the problem now to some time in the future when hopefully it will cease to be a problem. Using A3 paper as a large canvas, draw a window of six panes of roughly equal size. From top left to bottom right number the panes progressively from 1 to 6 (see Figure 8.10). You can choose either to use words to describe the problem in the top-left box, or to draw a picture in cartoon form showing how you perceive the problem. Whatever choice is made, the exercise is repeated in the last bottom-right box but this time describing in words or illustrating by cartoon what you wish to see as an ultimate solution or desired state. Between box 1 and box 6 there are four blank spaces to be filled with words or cartoons as a means of showing how the current situation can move from problem to solution. There is a built-in assumption here that four discrete steps are needed to get from problem to solution, but there is no need to confine the steps to four – more or fewer may be used as needed by varying the size of the window.

Some people are discouraged from drawing cartoon-like pictures to illustrate their ideas because of an inability to draw. As with diagram-

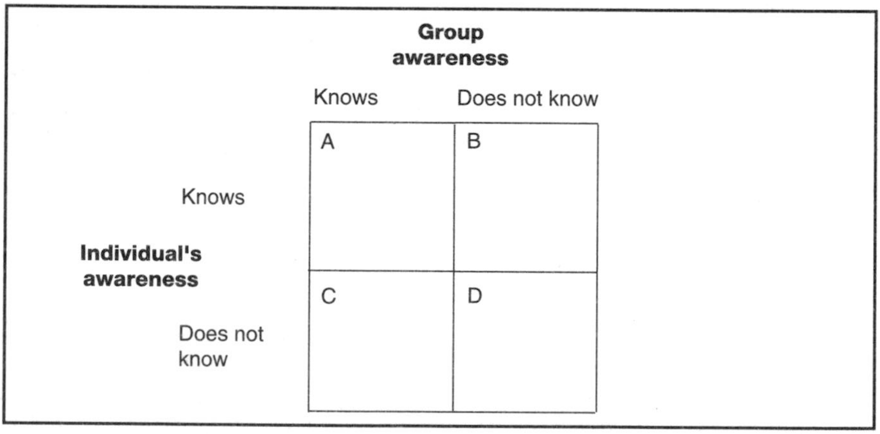

Figure 8.9 Window diagram of group/individual awareness

ming, we can all draw and can expect to improve this skill only through practice. Richard Feynman (see the Bibliography), a Nobel prize-winning scientist who died in 1988, once described how, on alternate Sundays, an artist friend taught him about art and drawing while he taught the artist about science. Feynman started by saying he could never draw, but went on to become an artist himself. The work that gained him the Nobel prize included drawings that became known as the Feynman Diagrams, which contain visually the same information as the original mathematics.

The only way to draw is to drop any inhibitions and just do it. Again, as pointed out earlier with reference to diagrams, there is no need to produce masterpieces, because the cartoon story-board is a temporary aid to thinking and can be discarded when the work is done. A cartoon story-board can look like the diagram in Figure 8.10. This form of diagram has been developed by Jane Henry at the Open University Business School.

The early cave drawings found particularly in Australia, but other areas too, were 'read' by people who could not read or write in the conventional meaning of the words. For the beginner, stick people can be drawn, and to exercise the imagination, symbols can be drawn to represent ideas. There are some standard symbols to help us represent ideas or behaviour, which, unlike tangible objects, are sometimes difficult to capture graphically. The exercise of drawing images to get your feelings about an issue down on paper can be almost therapeutic.

As previously described in Table 3.1, crossed swords can show conflict, a light-bulb is quite well known as a symbol for ideas, tangled rope for

Figure 8.10   Window diagram of cartoon story-board showing a work-pressure problem

complexity, a brick wall for being obstructive and so on. When drawn in the context of the cartoon such symbols can carry considerable meaning.

A diagram of this kind, whether by cartoon or words, can encourage other people to 'read into' what they see and to offer more images to the cartoon or words to the story-board. This is another example of a diagram providing a broad, at-a-glance, view of a complex subject. An alternative is to write into the Window diagram to form what has become known as a 'story-board'. The diagram in Figure 8.11 shows how this can be done. This is a written version of Figure 8.10, but someone 'reading' the cartoon version may see more than has been expressed in words alone.

Think about how the Window diagram can be used to throw light on difficult issues. The ideal number of 'panes' to work with seems to be between, and including, four to sixteen. The majority of situations can be captured within this range.

Business purpose of the Window diagram

- Whenever there is a two-sided, or many-sided, debate, conflict or issue in business think about how the Window diagram could be used to capture essential relationships which in turn throw light on what seems initially to be a confused situation.
- When a problem seems to defy solution, a good idea is to represent the current situation graphically, then immediately leap to what can be visualized as an ideal situation. As shown here this can be done by moving from window pane 1 to pane 6. When steps towards the ideal are being drawn it may be necessary to extend, or reduce, the number of panes depending upon the extent of the problem.
- There is a clear purpose in capturing key aspects of a new idea or new product in one all-embracing diagram. From this stage it is comparatively easy to see alternative actions, or think of ways to reinforce the strength of an idea, as well as thinking how to remove or avoid weaknesses.

Summary and conventions

In summary, the Window diagram is a very versatile tool because a wide range of circumstances can be captured within the area of a window. The scope is limited only by the size of available 'canvas'. Although the most common practice is to use words and story-board, it is really beneficial to use cartoons as well. The picture does not have to

1	2	3
Problem: Work just keeps on piling up, out of control, boss always complaining. Really getting me down – feel shackled to this problem with no clear means of escape.	No clear way of unlocking this problem. However, having thought about it a good deal I am beginning to grow in confidence and feel there could be a solution.	The more I look at the problem the key seems to be use of time.
4	5	6
Metaphorically – need more sand in the glass of Old Father Time – must find some way of doing this.	Also need to look at my image and not working smart enough, and must be strongly willing to get more time.	Written this straight after box 1. The ideal picture is one of me still having to juggle many things but doing it in a relaxed way while still being a demanding game.

Figure 8.11 Window diagram of story-board describing a work-pressure problem

be expertly drawn to demonstrate imagination or insight; and the roughest sketch can convey a message worth very many words.

Conventions for the Window diagram

- Begin by thinking of two-by-two situations.
- Recognize connections between the respective sides (top and left).
- Key words for sides of each box can be used.
- Describe typical situations/images that can fit into each box.
- 'Push' the diagram by thinking of alternative key words to generate other ideas.
- Think of how you can develop larger windows for more complex situations.
- Drop any inhibitions to draw pictorial images within the Window diagram.

9 Thinking about flow

Flow-Process and Flow-Block diagrams

The core Flow diagram consists of boxes and / or bubbles linked together with arrows that show direction of flow. The convention is that flow moves either left to right across the page or from top to bottom. The exception is when feedback is drawn as flowing from right to left or bottom to top. Boxes are used to indicate clear objective statements that are measurable in some way while blobs are used for more subjective statements containing less certainty. One critical feature that helps differentiate between types of Flow diagram is whether verbs and nouns are used throughout in a consistent way, as in the Flow-Process diagram, Figure 9.1, or only nouns are used, as in the Flow-Block diagram in Figure 9.2. It does make sense to have consistency in the way boxes are described.

There are steps: A then B then C etc. to the central part of this diagram; one event must finish before the next can begin. This is a fundamental feature of all Flow diagrams, and simply reflects common sense. The upper and lower parts of the diagram in Figure 9.1 demonstrate how two tasks can be combined at the same time: the oven is heating while the ingredients and cake are prepared and washing can be done while baking takes place.

From this simple explanation it should not be too difficult to see how more complicated processes can follow the same principle. The steps become more numerous and two or more activities may take place with one step. The Flow-Block diagram, in contrast, is at a simpler level where the various bits and pieces involved in a process are shown as nouns. One diagram, on process, reflects what has to be done, while the other shows what is involved.

While flow is normally associated with streams, oil pipelines or beer pumps, the diagram can be drawn to illustrate a wide range of processes. The Flow diagram can be used for showing a sequence of logical thought, information flow, traffic movement, sequence of

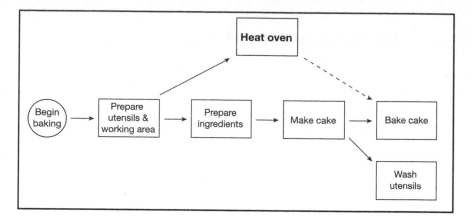

Figure 9.1　Basic Flow-process diagram

decision-making, planning a computer programme, a wedding or a survey questionnaire.

Various names are given to diagrams that are essentially flow diagrams by their nature, and this helps differentiate between types of Flow diagram. However, they all have common characteristics. All are concerned with sequencing, or steps, something is passing from one state to the next. Various symbols are used as a form of shorthand and at times more than one task can occur within the same step.

When diagramming flow there is a start event and a finish event. In between there are intermediate events that occur at the end of each activity. Events and activities can be drawn in three standard ways, shown below.

1. Activity on node (AON)
2. Event on node (EON)
3. Activity on arrow (AOA)

Each approach to showing events and activities has its own advocates, but in practice the important thing is to communicate the essential

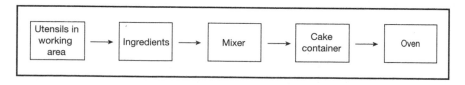

Figure 9.2　Basic Flow-Block diagram

features of flow as the drawer sees them. Having a choice between approaches simply adds to your diagramming repertoire.

There are two main features of the activity-on-arrow diagram: the event or node and the activity (see Figure 9.3).

An event is the condition that begins a particular activity and signals its completion. In the AOA diagram this is shown by small circles referred to as nodes. The convention is to show the activity above the arrow, and time below as in Figure 9.3. The time can be in any units: minutes, hours, days, weeks or months, but must be consistent throughout the diagram. The length of arrow is not related to time in this diagram, and different thickness of arrow is not used in any Flow diagram. Arrows are drawn proportionate to time only in the time-based-activity-on-arrow (TBAOA) diagram. In this diagram the arrows are drawn to scale in accordance with the time taken between nodes.

One difficulty in setting Flow diagrams in the context of this book is that drawing them can be a very 'mechanical' activity. There can be simply a recording of what is happening, and this is little more than an administrative task. The thinking part of handling these diagrams has to come from allowing the diagrams to 'speak to us'. 'What does this picture of boxes and arrows in a line tell us about what is going on?' 'Is there a better configuration?' 'What could be missing?' 'Is it worth applying another type of diagram to the process?' These questions and more ought to spring out of Flow diagrams if they are to be used as tools for thought rather than as routine administration.

BUSINESS APPLICATION OF THE FLOW DIAGRAM

The diagram in Figure 9.4 shows a Flow-Process diagram for the task of designing a questionnaire, and then conducting a survey. Such surveys are used with customers, prospective customers, employees and the wider public.

A survey, of any kind, is a notoriously easy process to get wrong; problems can occur at each step which are not normally detected until

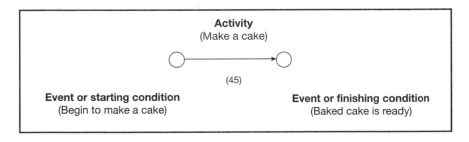

Figure 9.3 Simple activity on arrow diagram (time in minutes)

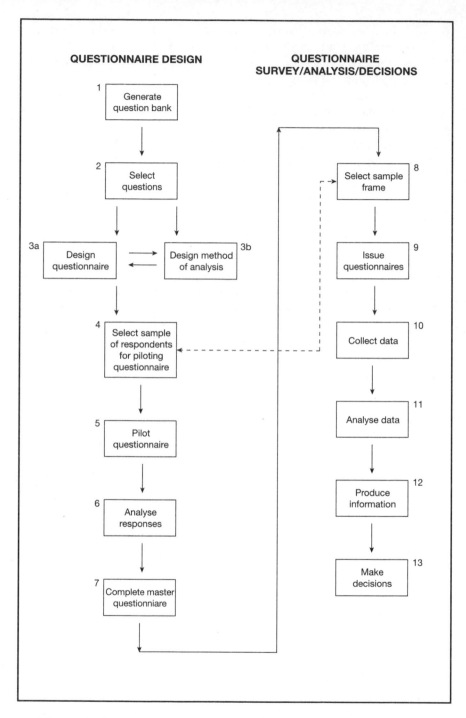

Figure 9.4 Flow-process diagram of questionnaire design, survey, analysis and decisions

much later, when it can be too late to correct any errors. A good example is when the questionnaire is designed without taking account of how the answers are, eventually, to be analysed. Difficulties that arise at the time of analysis, such as the questioning method not being consistent with the chosen analysis method, means that the problem cannot be resolved, because the questions have already been asked. It is for this reason that two activities, shown in boxes 3a and 3b, interact concurrently at the design stage. This diagram reflects a process that requires considerable thought before anything is done, and Flow diagramming is an invaluable aid to thinking through each step of the way. Looking at the diagram in Figure 9.4 and step 1, we can think about where the most appropriate questions will come from and who will provide them, and how we will know they are valid. What collection of people will fit into the sample frame at step 8? What sample can be used for the pilot questionnaire, steps 4 and 5, and how does this relate to the actual survey sample of people at step 8? The dotted line indicates a task that cannot be done in sequence. The pilot sample must reflect the eventual sample to be used, but before the final sample frame has been designed. Could the two kinds of sample be done concurrently? Questions and ideas can be bubbling up as this diagram is drawn, and notes can be made alongside each stage to help form a full picture of the work to be done.

BUSINESS PURPOSES OF THE FLOW DIAGRAM

- The Flow diagram normally reflects well-ordered sequential business activity. This overall picture can lead to fixed patterns of thought about the activity in question; too easily the Flow diagram can reflect mindsets. More productive use can be made of this type of diagram by letting it 'speak' to the drawer or reader. Ask what the diagram is telling you about critical relationships between steps or between activities. 'Can the diagram be drawn differently to achieve a more efficient process?' Use both Process and Block diagram where it is necessary to capture a complete picture of what is involved. Experiment with different patterns of flow. Practise a form of pictorial brainstorming, and allow patterns of seemingly impossible flows, as a means of arriving at a previously elusive solution.
- Although there are many computer software aids to project management, providing Flow diagrams, there can be great value and convenience in having the skill to draw and manipulate different types of Flow diagram by hand. There is the creative use of drawing, using mind and hand in tandem, and the convenience of being able to do this spontaneously, anywhere. The purpose here is to use Flow

diagrams actively as tools for thought, rather than as a recipe-type approach to tasks at work.

SUMMARY AND CONVENTIONS

In summary, and looking back to the diagrams in this section, the first (Figure 9.1) is an activity-on-node (AON) diagram; the next (Figure 9.2) is an event-on-node (EON) diagram; and the third (Figure 9.3) is an activity-on-node diagram. This placing of activities on the node is the approach more commonly favoured at the present time. However, this is to facilitate planning and the writing of programmes for computer use. In terms of thinking, it is the activity-on-arrow type that seems to offer more scope, especially when combined with drawing of arrows to a scale that represents time. The drawing and thinking through activity-on-arrow diagrams (AOA), the third method listed on p. 000 is most appropriate to behaviours that take place in a kind of linked network, not unlike Beck's London Underground diagram where transport flow is the subject. It is this kind of Flow diagram we will consider in the next section.

Conventions for Flow-Process and Flow-Block diagrams

- Flow moves from left to right or top to bottom unless feedback is included.
- Boxes are used for objective measurable activities, bubbles for subjective items.
- Activity can be described at the node or on an arrow.
- Events are start- or finish-points for each activity included in the diagram.
- With activities on the arrows, the events are at the nodes.

FLOW IN NETWORKS

The Flow diagrams considered so far have been of the step-by-step or staged nature of flow, like a stream meeting on its way various 'events' such as a dam, waterfall or pond. Networks occur when there is more than one flow to think about, which may form a pattern more like the Nile Delta than the River Thames. Various names are given to a number of diagramming methods designed to handle flow:

Algorithm
Activity-Sequence
Flow-Block

Flow-Process
Critical Path Analysis (CPA)
Critical Path Method (CPM)
Program Evaluation Review Technique (PERT)
Ring

Probably the best known is the critical path method (CPM) – see Moder (1983) – which is the overall technique of drawing diagrams to show a network with start, finish, and intermediate stages, and showing activities and/or events according to the chosen method. The associated technique of critical path analysis (CPA), as the name implies, is concerned with breaking down the network into measurable chunks and devising ways to measure the flow of activities. The analysis of these measures provides information on early/late starts or finishes, duration of each activity and any inbuilt float or slack in the time between nodes. A comprehensive coverage of this subject has been provided by Lockyer and Gordon (1991).

BUSINESS APPLICATION OF THE FLOW IN NETWORK DIAGRAM

The fundamental idea in Flow diagrams of one activity finishing before the next begins can become less obvious in a network. Consider the diagram in Figure 9.5 for example. The diagram is telling us that:

activity A must be completed before activities B and C can begin;
activity B before activity D and activity C before E;
activities D and E before G, and activity D before F;
activity F before H, and G before I, Activities H and I before J.

A dotted line in an AOA diagram indicates what is called a dummy activity and shows that one event precedes another but that no activity is

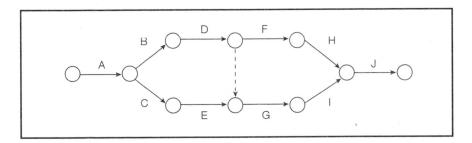

Figure 9.5   Action-on-arrow Network-Flow diagram

necessary. In Figure 9.5 this dummy is showing that both D and E are necessary before G begins, but F relies only on D. If the dotted arrow was reversed then both D and E would precede F.

From the core diagram example given here it should be noted that there is no feedback loop from one node back to another node. A little thought makes you realize that for diagrams used in the CPM, feedback becomes invalid, because the statement is saying that a node precedes another node in time when the other node or event has already happened.

Each node can contain information about timing of activities and identification of the node itself. There are a number of ways that this information can be presented, but generally the most common and simplest is to divide the node into three sections to show the three items of information.

The EET is the Earliest Event Time, the earliest time that the event can happen. This is the earliest time that activities leaving the node can begin.

The LET is the latest event time, the latest time that the event can happen, if the overall objective is to be achieved. This is the latest time that activities entering the node can finish.

This is the basic 'mechanics' of a Network-Flow diagram. The thinking is done when the events have to be made clear and the activities have to be sequenced in an optimum way. The sequencing can be helped by numbering the nodes 1, 2, 3 etc. from left to right and the simple way is to place a rule vertically and move it across the diagram from the beginning, numbering the nodes as they appear.

There is a direct link between the drawing of Network-Flow diagrams and objective Trees, described in Chapter 3. The termination point of a Network diagram should be an objective, and it is essential that this is clearly defined before the diagramming begins. As the saying goes, if you do not know where you are going, any road will take you there – so a Network diagram is unnecessary. The activities on the arrows equate with the options listed on the objective Tree, or the means of getting from one sub-objective (node) to another until the final objective has been reached. An objective Tree as shown in Figure 5.4 is a very useful way to begin thinking about the drawing of a Network diagram. The one criticism of using a preliminary diagram of this kind is that the task can help to form a mindset about what is to be done, but there are ways to avoid this. From reading this book it ought to be clear that no diagram is set in stone – they are highly fluid creations. Any firm ideas about which activities are most critical need to be shelved until the network-type Flow diagram is complete. Any pre-judgement is to be avoided before a diagramming session; the complete picture must be allowed to tell its own story. The objective Tree is a very useful way, initially, to provide direction.

As with all diagramming it is important to keep networks as simple as possible, the aim is to find the simplest route through a task with a minimum of detail. In using diagrams of this kind the timescale is realistically in weeks rather than months, and very rarely years. Normally, far too much change is likely to occur beyond a period of months, and an elaborate tightly planned diagram will usually prove to be too optimistic over this longer time-frame.

BUSINESS PURPOSES OF THE FLOW IN NETWORK DIAGRAM

- Most activity in business is of the network type, and mirrors nature as being like a spider web, branches of a tree or mountain streams; they all have complex patterns and are ever changing: change is an integral part of all business activity and to understand the various patterns and how they change it is helpful to have a way of capturing them on paper. The purpose of Flow in Network diagrams is to show patterns of network-type activity and how the activity changes over time.
- Generally, the activity on arrow allows us to visualize more clearly what is going on between events and, most importantly, provides a pattern of activity in sequence and in tandem where various permutations of options may be considered. Even the most established practices can be thought about in different ways from time to time, and the Network-Flow diagram helps stimulate thinking about a variety of possibilities.

SUMMARY AND CONVENTIONS

In conclusion, the Network diagram ought to encourage you to ask 'what-if' questions about each activity and about the pattern of relationships that are apparent from the picture in front of you. What if these three activities could be amalgamated? What if some float or slack was built into this activity? What if we brought this event forward? Many questions can be generated from inspection of a complete diagram or even during the act of drawing. The diagrams presented under the banner of 'Flow' tend to be seen essentially as tools for planning, but they do have a valuable part to play in prompting thought and ideas.

Conventions for Flow in Network diagrams

- Flow is across the page left to right.
- Feedback (right to left) is an invalid condition.
- Activity on node or activity on arrow can be used.
- Numbers can be used at the Node to give earliest event time and latest event time, plus node identification.
- A dotted arrow (dummy) can be used to show one event preceding another where no activity is involved.

The Algorithm

The principle of flow applies here too, but a flow that is largely governed by a series of questions and responses. The direction of arrows is especially critical to this type of diagram because quite complicated paths can be followed through some algorithms. The convention is to omit arrows for straight downward flow: the direction is taken as read. Flows across the page or feedback loops need to have their direction shown by arrows. The Algorithm diagram normally appeals to people who prefer to think in a serialist way; each step relies totally upon the preceding step, which means it ought to be welcomed by mathematicians too. All extraneous influences can be ignored, so the aim is to include only items essential to the process being described. Very specific 'closed' questions are asked that can only be given the answer 'yes' or 'no' and these are written within diamond shapes. Activities are also written in a very specific way and enclosed in boxes. The conventional circle is used to start the algorithm. (See Table 3.1, showing building blocks of diagrams.)

The example shown in Figure 9.6 is simple, but the same principle applies to all Algorithm diagrams: there is a course of action that has been planned and sideways movement takes account of anticipated possibilities. This type of diagram serves a useful function when situations are reasonably predictable. When the unexpected occurs you need alternative tools. In this queuing example there is an assumption that if two or three people are together only one person will be buying a ticket, so even though there may be more people in one queue than another, the processing time could be less because there are fewer purchases of tickets. However, this takes no account of many other factors, such as groups who do buy separate tickets, or people with problems. A

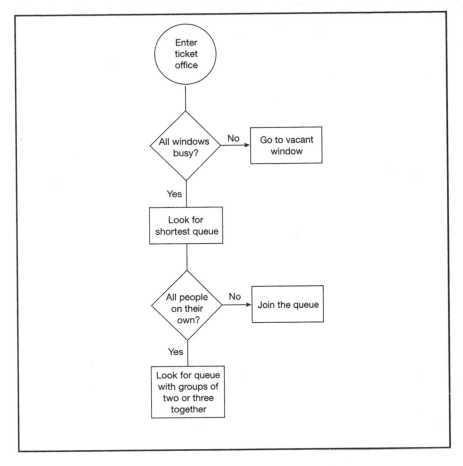

Figure 9.6 Algorithm (simple example)

comprehensive algorithm to serve this purpose would need to include the facility for questioning people in the queue. We may doubt whether it is being realistic to expect a queue-selection algorithm that would produce results better than chance, so we are left with random selection and, yes, we always chose the wrong queue.

BUSINESS APPLICATION OF THE ALGORITHM DIAGRAM

In Figure 9.7 we return to our GP example from earlier chapters and see how an Algorithm diagram can demonstrate a typical diagnosis session with a patient. Inspection of the diagram reveals that questions are contained within a diamond-shape and activities are in boxes, which is the convention. The yes or no answer is entered after each diamond, and the activity follows according to the kind of response. The point needs to be

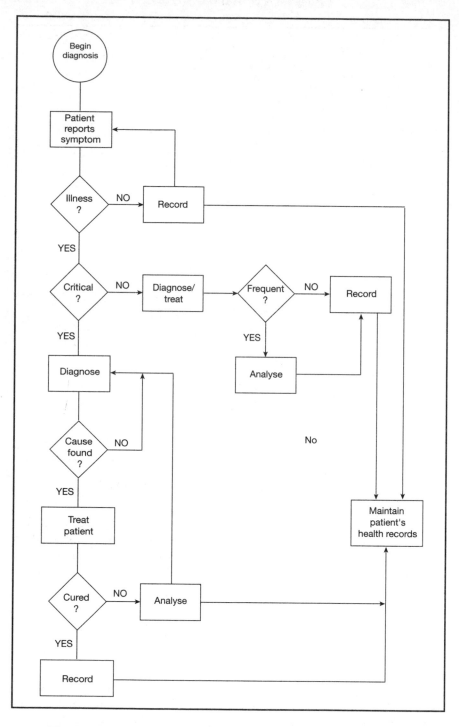

Figure 9.7   Algorithm diagram of diagnosis in a GP's practice
(example only)

made again that questions must be closed, that is, they are asked in such a way that only a yes or no answer is possible. This narrow questioning means, inevitably, that the breakdown of the task has to be in small chunks and must be very precise. The activity described in each box needs to be clear and concise; note from Figure 9.7 how all boxes include a verb such as 'record', 'maintain' or 'treat' in each short statement.

A number of ideas can arise when exploring the diagram, for instance, that the symptom reported is not necessarily the actual symptom, so possibly an additional investigative loop could be added to check the accuracy of the reported symptom. There are no feedback loops out of the patient's health record – where could they go if drawn in? Even non-critical illness could become more critical, so the analysis box following the question 'frequent?' (yes or no), could possibly go further than to record.

Although directed towards the running of a medical business, this diagram could equally be applied to any task where a problem needs to be diagnosed. The word 'symptom' can be substituted by the term 'problem awareness', and the word 'illness' by 'problem'; then, instead of asking 'critical?', the question can read 'major or minor?'. The remainder of the diagram dealing with cause can be followed as read with the exception of 'taking action' rather than 'treating'. This diagram has been used as a model for designing a fault diagnosis system in manufacturing, where reliability is critical and efficient fault records must be well maintained.

BUSINESS PURPOSES OF THE ALGORITHM DIAGRAM

The main purpose in business is to set out a clear sequence of steps that takes into account, as far as possible, variations that can occur. When deviations are discovered that have not been covered, they are simply built into the diagram to make it a live ongoing tool.

- Use this type of diagram whenever there is a series of 'if this, then this' steps to reaching a solution. Although most commonly encountered in vehicle or other repair manuals, the Algorithm ought to be applied more widely in business. There can be disadvantages when people become too reliant upon the method, principally when an event happens outside the scope of the Algorithm, leaving the Algorithm-user without a strategy, or without being practised in going outside the strict confines of the diagram. On the other hand, as a support to other problem-solving methods the Algorithm is of great value.
- When drawing an Algorithm diagram it is rare for an accurate picture to be produced quickly or at a first attempt. Normally a good deal of trial and error is necessary. It is wise to begin at the beginning and decide upon the end before deciding which steps fill the

gap between. The conventions listed below need to be followed because like normal conventions in writing they aid clear communication between people. The main purpose in business is to set out a clear sequence of steps that takes into account, as far as possible, variations that can occur. When deviations are discovered that have not been covered, they are simply built into the diagram to make it a live ongoing tool.

SUMMARY AND CONVENTIONS

In summary, the Algorithm diagram is a very good tool for gaining an overview of how experts or skilled people go about their tasks. When such people do something different as a result of asking themselves a question and finding an answer, the actual reasoning may be known only to them. In some cases the decision can be viewed by outsiders as an example of genius when in practice they are following a personally well-worn path of reasoning. Drawing an Algorithm diagram helps to tease out the line of reasoning that leads eventually to the decision. An Algorithm diagram can be no more than an outline in this sense because it is limited to closed questions, but nevertheless it is a potentially valuable outline. Most thinking is done when it is possible to elaborate on each step of the diagram, and explore, in more depth, the reasons given for making the yes or no responses. For example, in Figure 9.6, what criteria are used to decide on 'critical' or 'not critical'? Interrogation of the Algorithm diagram can reveal a good deal about what is called expert knowledge.

Conventions for the Algorithm diagram

- Use accepted symbols, that are conventional, for start, activities and decisions.
- Use only closed questions.
- Arrows are only necessary when working across or up the page.
- Activity needs to be clear, concise, and to include a verb.

The Ring diagram

The core diagram given here is a very common image wherever diagrams are used regularly. At some time the familiar wheel-like picture will be produced. The Ring diagram has a long history; there are examples of it in medieval times where stages were recorded in the wheel of life. The diagrams included rich pictures to help illustrate the different stages. Now that you should have more familiarity with diagramming, the idea of incorporating a rich picture into a Ring diagram is something you may like to attempt.

One key feature of this diagram is that you always finish where you began. The saying about running around like headless chickens could be apt, but this would be unkind to what is a very useful diagram. The diagram in this form represents flow of activity in discrete stages, but where the actions in one stage lead naturally into the next. Unlike most Flow diagrams there is not necessarily a complete finishing of one stage before the next begins; 'blending' is probably the best word to describe the linkage of stages. The Ring diagram is suitable for tasks where you need to learn from the act of going around the ring once in order to be better prepared for when the process is repeated. Regular or irregular events come to mind, such as organizing a carnival or show annually, or a company going through a process of change from time to time, but with no fixed timescale. Chemical plants often shut down every three to five years and the restart procedure can present the same problems that occurred three or more years earlier, and the same number of years before that. From shut down to restart is an example of going through a process and finishing in the state where you began. In this example there is a cycle of events that can be captured very well by the Ring diagram. When a company goes periodically through a reorganization,

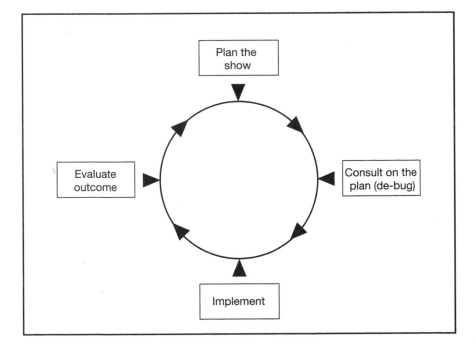

Figure 9.8 Basic Ring diagram of a show operation

changes take place, but from the beginning of the reorganization to completion is a cycle where people arrive back where they began, only now in a fitter state.

The most basic Ring diagram covers four stages (Figure 9.8). The aim is to arrive back at 12 o'clock ready to start again as a wiser show-organizer, even though the next opportunity may be almost twelve months away. The millennium event organizers can scrap any Ring diagrams they have used in planning.

The diagram is not limited to four stages, though the usual steps of 360 divisions in the circle are rather too many for practical purposes. The average is around six stages and there are rarely over ten.

BUSINESS APPLICATIONS OF THE RING DIAGRAM

There can be around ten stages to the task of carrying out a major change, depending upon how involved the process is likely to be. What can be considered to be a core Ring diagram for a change process is shown in Figure 9.9.

There are times when a diagram of this kind begins at a stage where

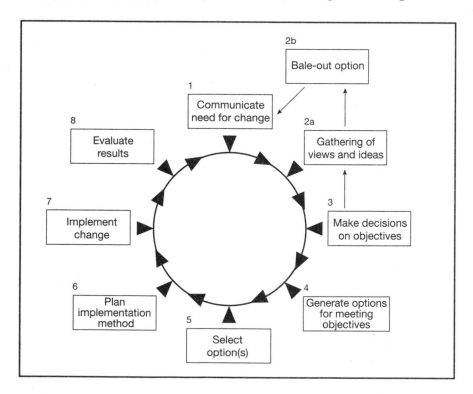

Figure 9.9   Ring diagram for managing change

the decision to change has already been made and any consultation is only about how to change and not *whether* to change. Managing change ought to include the option of 'not to change' as shown by step 2b in the diagram. In any deliberation about planned change there needs to be a baling-out option if, after consultation, this is seen to be the wisest decision. The diagram ought to make us think about the wisdom of going forward with change because being wise, or not wise, becomes an integral part of the whole process, and needs to be taken into account at the evaluation stage. A comment such as 'in hindsight we should have remained as we were' may be heard in relation to change. This would be said at or after step 8, when it is then too late.

Thinking about change leads to some elaboration of the basic four-stage diagram. In Figure 9.9 this has already begun with eight stages and four feedback loops. A loop is drawn between stage 3 and stage 2a, because if people are asked for views and ideas it is critical that their contribution is acknowledged. Then from stage 2a to 2b is very important, because many changes are carried out with the decision to change having been already decided. The loop from 2b to the beginning allows for the option of 'no change'. The fourth feedback from stage 6 to stage 3 is often referred to as iteration because it means not just feedback, but going back again to check that the objectives stated at stage 3 are still being followed in the implementation plan.

Figure 9.10 is a diagram quickly approaching overload: little more can be added without upsetting the aim of simplicity. However, important components have been brought into the picture. Ideally the central player, or (with possibly less impact) a group or team, maintains ongoing interaction with each stage of the process without necessarily being involved in an operational sense. Having these lines of interaction in the diagram makes us think about how the central individual(s) should handle each stage.

Around the outside we have examples of diagrams that could be used to help generate and communicate ideas and actions more clearly. The selection of diagrams is not absolute, but those listed are considered to be most suitable, especially where time is critical.

The thought may have occurred to you that there appears to be little difference between a Ring diagram and a Flow-Process diagram with feedback – see Figure 9.11.

The Flow-Process diagram, an example of activity on node (AON), is quite workable as an alternative approach to the Ring diagram. The main difference, however, is that the flow process reflects thinking about feedback when the process has been completed, whereas the Ring diagram reflects a continuous learning process that leads naturally back to the beginning, with no need for specific feedback from step 8 to step 1. On balance the Ring diagram is preferable where iteration as well as

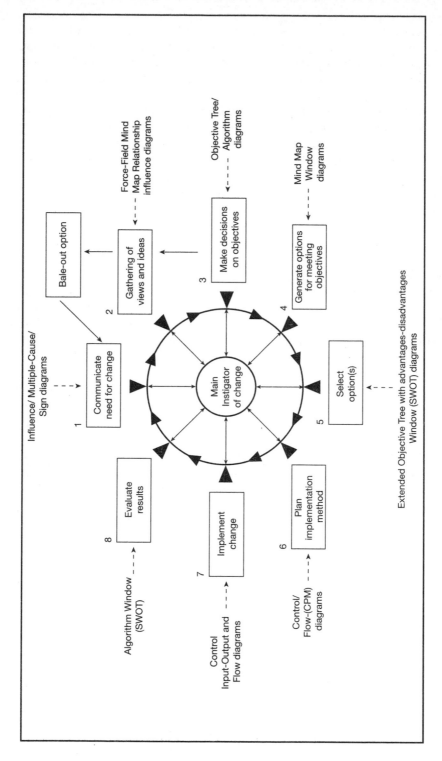

Figure 9.10 Ring diagram of change process with core diagrams shown

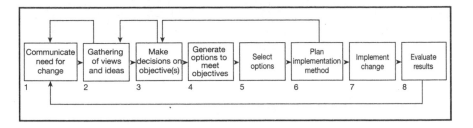

Figure 9.11 Flow-process diagram of change

feedback is needed and where ongoing learning at each stage is important. In all situations where major change takes place there ought to be at least one person who ultimately drives the process, and it is easier to show this role within a Ring diagram.

BUSINESS PURPOSE OF THE RING DIAGRAM

The main purpose of a Ring diagram in business is to provide a way of emphasizing the often encompassing nature of human activity. There is a distinction between activity that makes changes to what is done, and activity that changes something completely. A manufacturing process converts raw materials into a product that can show a complete change from the original state. Making changes to a process involving human behaviour is not like this; some aspects of behaviour can be changed, while others cannot. All change of this kind involves arriving back at the human state, possibly changed in some way but not completely. In the Ring diagram, the actual change does not occur until step 7, so there has been much human activity to determine what can and what cannot be done before this stage is reached. The Ring also helps to show a central controlling person who is in a strategic position rather than involved operationally. There is feedback to this person at each step of the change, and the role is not unlike that of a comparator in a control process (see Control diagram in Figure 6.5). The central figure provides a vital link between those making the change and the strategic reasons for proposing the change.

SUMMARY AND CONVENTIONS

In summary, the Flow diagram can take many forms, as demonstrated in this chapter. Whatever the kind of flow, or the pattern that is adopted for arrows and symbols, there are fundamental principles to be followed, as outlined here. These principles are concerned with the mechanics of producing Flow diagrams, essentially a series of tasks of an administrative type. The Ring diagram, presented last, has the important difference of a blending between stages, where activities can run into each other. In this sense the diagram is less prescriptive than the Flow diagrams shown earlier, which makes the Ring more appropriate in situations where there is much human involvement, such as planning a major change.

Conventions for the Ring diagram

- Begin with four stages and fill in additional stages as necessary.
- Keep it as simple as possible.
- Note the difference between iteration and feedback.
- Make use of iteration and feedback as necessary.
- Further thinking can lead to an elaboration of the diagram.
- When applied to managing change, include a central person.

PART III

Overview: Managing
Information, Theory and Pitfalls

10 Managing information using Core diagrams

Mountains or tides of information

A number of metaphors can be used to illustrate the amount of information to be managed in present-day business. One is of a tide that keeps sweeping over organizations, always increasing in height. Another metaphor is of an information mountain that when scaled is found to have a very short level ridge leading to an even higher mountain. The first example reflects helplessness, while the other shows a desire to keep on top of the information growth. However we wish to view information, it is unrealistic to expect either the tide to grow less, or the final mountain top to be climbed.

Information comes to us in many forms: by the spoken word face to face or electronically, by the written word as hard copy or electronically, or by graphic representation as hard copy or electronically. Normally a distinction is made between data, information and knowledge. 'Data' refers to a collection of facts that have yet to be interpreted.

If, for example, a company is interested in the relationship between the packaging design of a product and sales, it is the actual relationship, or more precisely the kinds of influence between design and sales they wish to know about, and in their own context. Much data could be accessed on how design A increases sales Y, or how design A is better than design B in increasing sales Y. This is an example of data, which need to be interpreted to provide useful information, taking into account context and other possible independent variables, before arriving finally at a state of knowing about the relationship between design and sales. When some interpretation has been given to data they become information, and from information we gain knowledge or the ability 'to know'. Managing information effectively usually means extracting essential bits that allows us to be knowledgeable at any one time. Samuel Johnson, according to Boswell's *Life*, said, 'Knowledge is of two kinds. We know a subject ourselves, or we know where we can find information upon it.'

The exponential growth in information has led, especially in the

United States, to the occupation of information brokers. For any one company, an information broker will go m ining in a mountain of information to extract what that company needs to know. The main source of brokers is the Burwell World Directory of Information Brokers with almost 2000 entries in 1997.

Core diagrams have a role to play in managing information; a recent paper by William Rouse (1998) proposes knowledge maps for knowledge-mining and although this represents a very loose definition of a map, the idea is well worth pursuing. An alternative approach is to combine different core diagrams depending upon how you wish to manage information. It is common to discuss knowledge management, but essentially it is information that is being managed in order to extract the knowledge we need at any given time. Of all the data and/or information thrown at an organization, only a small amount will be needed to satisfy the need to know, or knowledge requirement.

When using core diagrams, we can ask questions such as:

a How is information controlled in this company?
b What influences determine the effectiveness and efficiency of our information handling?
c What causes problems in information handling?
d Where does information flow originate?
e How does information lead to possible changes?
f Where do we look to mine for knowledge?

Core diagrams that can be applied to these questions:

a Control diagram;
b Influence diagram;
c Multiple-Cause, Fishbone and Sign diagrams;
d System Map and/or Flow Process diagram;
e Multiple-cause, Influence and Ring diagrams;
f System Map or Mind Map.

The outcome from using core diagrams in this way could be modelled into one all-embracing diagram, to produce what would be called a 'mapping' exercise, but the result would be a very complex 'picture' similar to Aurelio Peccei's 'The Club of Rome' diagram that attempted to map the earth's resources and sustainability. The approach of using diagrams in tandem allows you to examine control, influence, cause and source as distinct issues. When this has been done it is easier to recognize a more complete picture of how information is handled in your organization.

Controlling information

How does an organization control the flow of information and extract only what is needed? How is knowledge-finding controlled when the information is not readily available?

The two questions represent different types of control; the first is looking for stability and negative feedback, in order to reduce the flow of information to cover only what is needed or the 'stable state', while the second is looking for more information as to where the essential knowledge can be found, or positive feedback (see p. 80 on business purposes of the Control diagram).

A company can have control of information represented by the diagram in Figure 10.1. Although complete in every detail this diagram can be seen as an oversimplification of a very complex process, in that there are more questions than answers. The choice of selection criteria and method of information-sifting are crucial parts of the control process. The diagram can be adapted as shown in Figure 10.2. Other diagrams can be brought in to help develop the idea of controlling information flow. The Objective Tree diagram is used to clarify the reasons for needing certain information and to establish the criteria, and the Influence diagram to show the areas to be prioritized in setting up a sifting process. Examples will be given later in this section.

Controlling the extraction of knowledge from the available sifted information is a separate process, and an example of this is given in Figure 10.3. The inputs into the process shown here need some explanation. The key-word search refers to a well known research technique that, with so much information to handle, ought to have wider application in business. The principle of using key words is central to the use of Mind Maps and System Maps, and indeed to all diagrammatic approaches. In any body of information there are key words that determine whether that information is relevant to a business or not. A business can have known key words that are crucial to the activities they perform, not empty buzzwords like much of the language of politicians, but words that carry real meaning for the business. A key-word search then becomes an important part of an information-sifting process.

The input of 'abstract service' refers to monthly issues of abstracts taken from various books and journals, the best known being ANBAR, but many professions have their own source of abstract publications. The main function performed by abstracts is to provide essential knowledge in a form that is concise and quick to absorb. A scan read allows one to know whether the complete book or article is worth accessing. No time is wasted in reading lengthy text that may not provide any added value in terms of knowledge gained.

The 'gatekeeper' role and networking inputs are closely linked. The

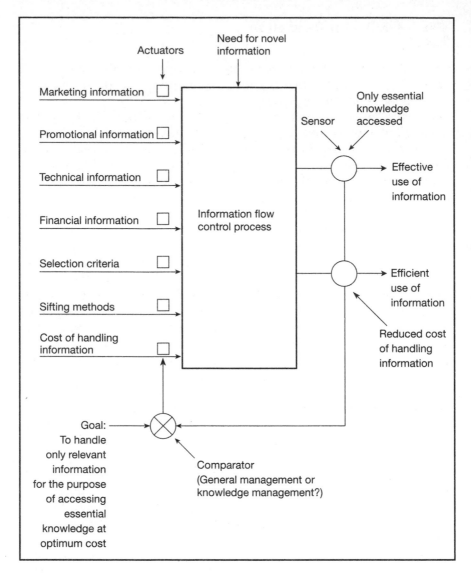

Figure 10.1 Standard control diagram for control of information

role is performed by a person who reaches out beyond the boundary of the business (for the concept of boundary see Chapter 4), knows about current and impending developments, reads business and/or technical journals and can act as sifter or gatekeeper in determining what the business ought to know. Sometimes a business is fortunate enough to have more than one person like this; some businesses are unfortunate in having none. People who fulfil this role also network a good deal, both in and out of the immediate workplace. Networking here refers to the

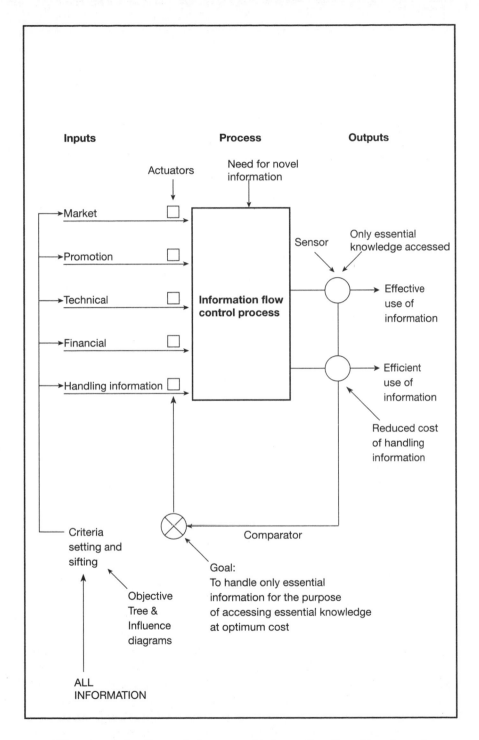

Figure 10.2 Control diagram of information flow (developed)

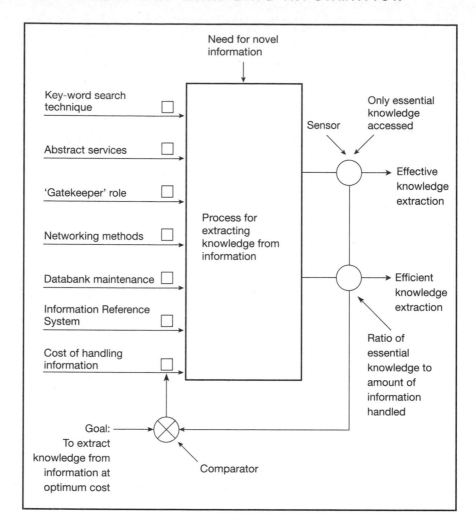

Figure 10.3   Control diagram of knowledge extraction

business activity of accessing knowledge through people, media, various sources of information and socially.

The data bank input is named this way because it is the common term in use, but in reality we should be calling it a knowledge bank – knowledge (as we have seen) is two steps away from data handling. In terms of using diagrams to help handle information we should be able to see a flow from data to interpretation, then to information and eventually to knowledge. Organizations where knowledge-management has become a feature of their work could consider using a knowledge-bank. This follows on from the managing of information in an institution (such as a bank) that is itself designed to allow rapid access to what needs to be known. Finally, the use of information-accessing techniques and removal of extraneous information can reduce the cost of information-handling, itself a most important issue.

Information overload and its causes

The core diagram of Multiple-Cause is a useful tool to examine possible sources of information overload. There are other influences, apart from causation, to be considered, such as customer needs, financial regulations, health and safety or competition. The sources of such influence, for any one company, can be captured very well in an Influence diagram, but what actually causes information overload is done more effectively with a Multiple-Cause diagram. The situation is not unlike a householder continually sandbagging against repeated flooding when it is the causes of the problem that ought to be addressed. Information is like water: we all need it, but the amount and the type required should be manageable.

The 'story' presented in Figure 10.4 is incomplete, but it is not too difficult to go on adding to this diagram. Take a piece of scrap paper and do this for your own situation. The diagram is sufficiently comprehensive to include a positive feedback closed loop; inspect the diagram and locate

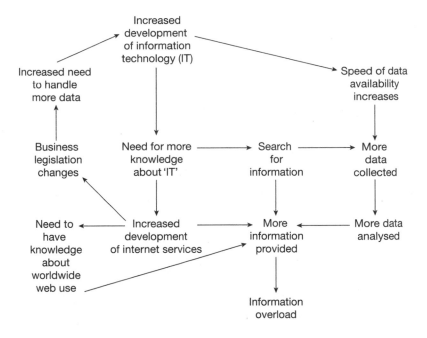

Figure 10.4   Multiple-cause diagram of information overload

where this is, and whether you feel it could be broken or have an intervention point introduced. There is unlikely to be one root cause of information overload: whenever a diagram is drawn, a web-like pattern emerges with one or more feedback loops with causes radiating out from any points in the loop. Some people argue that information overload is driven by technology. Because equipment can now handle greater amounts of information more quickly, greater amounts are generated. If this hypothesis could be supported, then just possibly we would have a root cause of the problem. The situation does appear to be far more complex, and many different demands for information, and ultimately knowledge, need to be understood if information is to be handled efficiently and effectively.

Mapping sources of information

The System Map shown in Figure 10.5 is based on one company and its boundary. The diagram ought to be self-explanatory, apart possibly from the central gatekeeper role, which we have just discussed (see p. 143). It spans out across the boundary to tap into the many sources of information identified by the diagram.

There is a difficult balance to be achieved between managing the flow

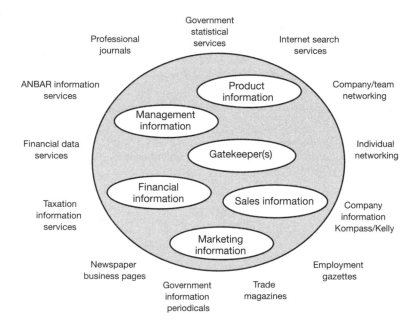

Figure 10.5 System map of information sources

of all information into the company, and gathering essential information when needed; one tends to be a defensive activity while the other is more outgoing and positive. In reality both approaches to information need to be outgoing, where the company takes charge of information flow, and this is essentially the job of people like gatekeepers.

Another way of looking at the management of information is to draw a Mind Map of what you and/or colleagues see as the step from very large amounts of information to the use of essential knowledge. Again, Figure 10.6 ought to be self-explanatory, although your Mind Map of the same subject may be quite different.

Summary

Managing information is at the root of diagram use whether for our own benefit or to communicate ideas to others. In this chapter we have considered how to use some core diagrams in the business of managing information itself. There is a dilemma in business between what can be described as an overload of available information on the one hand and an increasing need for essential information on the other, but the two are not necessarily incompatible. As Rouse (1998) points out, we do not make good use of available knowledge. 'The primary users are knowledge producers rather than knowledge consumers who tend to increase supply faster than demand.' When essential information is discussed the real debate is about knowledge, or the need to know. Before this 'knowing' stage is reached a great deal of available information may have been processed, at a cost. The case is presented here for using core diagrams as a means of understanding how information is managed in a series of activities. Asking how a business *controls* information is a fundamental question, and core diagrams can help us provide an answer. The act of diagramming can also lead to questions about the form of control in use, and to improvements in the method. Though information overload may be recognized it remains difficult to act on the problem unless critical causes have been identified. Normally 'information overload' is a statement of a symptom, and examination of causes should lead to a more meaningful description of the problem. The Multiple-Cause diagram is an ideal starting point to explore all possible causes of information overload. When a problem has been more clearly defined in a business, it can be written in the head of a Fishbone diagram and causes related to this problem prioritized (see an example of this diagramming in Chapter 7). Another approach, again described in Chapter 7, is to develop a Sign diagram around this problem and look in particular for key points of intervention.

The management of information can be mapped, using a System Map

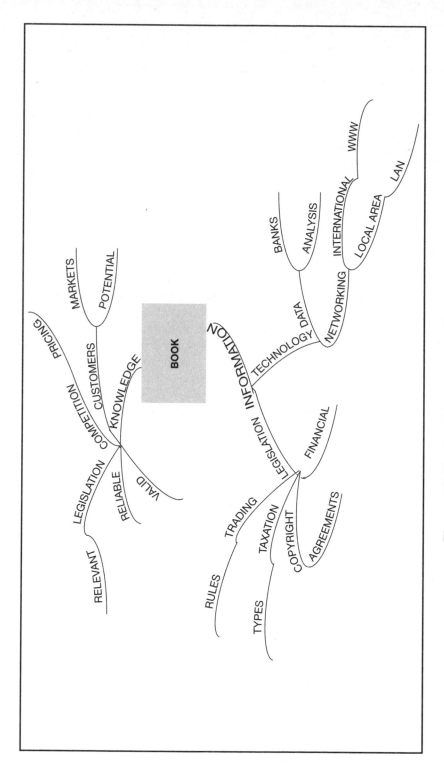

Figure 10.6 Mind Map of information management

and/or a Mind Map. The System Map aims to reflect what is out there and available, in other words it is a topographical map, while the Mind Map seeks to clarify relationships between all that is seen as being pertinent to the main central subject. When mapping information, these two approaches are complementary.

11 Diagramming theory and some pitfalls

Theory

It was Kurt Lewin (see p. 101) who said that there was nothing so practical as a good theory. He may well have added that even good theory tends to make more sense when you have experienced something of the practical first. Hopefully you will have seen practical uses of diagrams in Part 2 before reading this section.

There is a hidden hierarchy to the use of diagrams (see Figure 11.1), there is a movement from the general to the more specific as you pass from one type of diagram to another. This does not necessarily mean going 'deeper', because readers of any diagram may go as deep as they wish. The different levels relate to the specialization or 'focus' of any one diagram.

First, at the most generalist level, the System Map gives us a feel for the territory: the what, where and who of the subject being considered. A System Map provides an excellent overall snapshot by introducing the concept of boundary and making a clear distinction between inside-boundary and outside-boundary activity. In a nutshell, this map tells us what is involved and the position of the components relative to each other. This knowledge is not likely to solve problems, or produce new products, but does provide a broad systems view of a subject. The Mind Map in contrast is not essentially topographical because we look for associations between components, which then form groupings and links between groupings. In addition various symbols can be introduced and even directional arrows. The Relationship and Influence diagrams complete a set, that can be called 'generalist exploration'.

The high-flying aircraft in Figure 11.2 represents the generalist exploration in Figure 11.1 which aims to gain as wide a view as possible of a subject area, in a way similar to the System Map, Relationship and Influence diagrams. The Mind Map, in similar vein, extends the generalist theme by looking for associations between components in the diagram to aid memory and understanding of the selected central subject.

The lower-flying aircraft picks up the more specific detail in a way

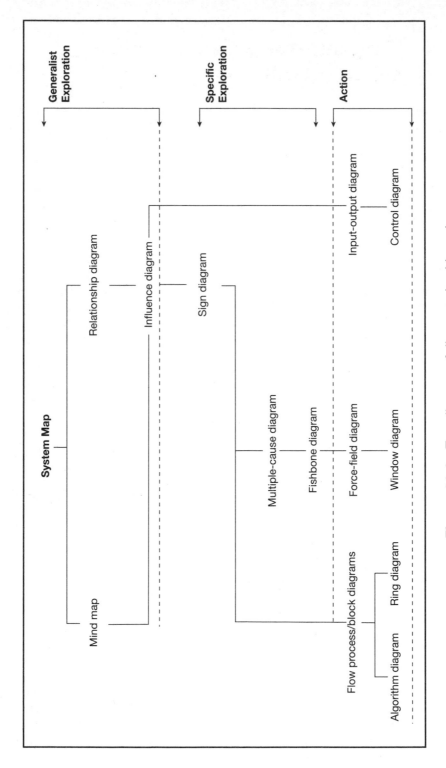

Figure 11.1 Tree diagram of diagramming hierarchy

similar to that of the three diagrams within the 'specific exploration' group. The moment arrows are introduced into a diagram, as in all Influence, Sign, Causal, Control and Force-Field diagrams (and some Mind Maps) we introduce more focus: first about direction and second about what it is that is being 'directed'. The introduction of arrows and signs on arrows, together with different configurations of components, enables much more specific analysis of a subject. Is it influence, is it cause, or flow? Any further speculation about type or strength of influence, or precise nature of a causal act, involves going deeper into the diagram, as illustrated by the arrows in Figure 11.2, but the focus remains the same.

The hierarchy continues through what can be described loosely as the 'arrow' diagrams. Of these the most generalist is the Influence diagram because it covers a broad sweep of behaviour within the term 'influence'. More focus is provided when signs are added to the arrows, because a specific statement is being made about the relationship between A at the tail of an arrow and B at the head. What happens at A will have either a positive (+), reinforcing influence on B, or a negative (–), opposite, and controlling influence.

The concept of multiple cause begins to move towards a more specific view of what may be happening, and when specific areas have been identified through the application of a Multiple-Cause diagram, the

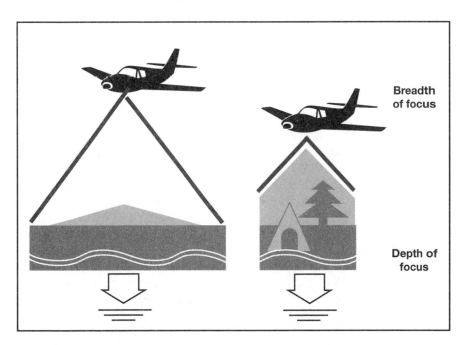

Figure 11.2   Rich picture of breadth of focus and depth of treatment

Fishbone diagram can bring an even clearer focus by considering a specific problem.

Flow-type diagrams (Force-Field, Window and Control) are all concerned with doing something: for example, Flow-type in planning a project, Force-Field in introducing a change, Window in developing a new product, and Control over a process.

In theory, diagrams do divide into functional groupings dictated by what can be achieved by drawing them. The outcomes can be enlightenment (from diagrams that promote exploration of ideas or simply of 'what is' in a given situation) or practical tangible results (from action prompted by the use of diagrams in a problem-solving way). There can be some confusion about what particular diagrams can and cannot achieve. Diagramming, that is making use of a range of diagrams together with the associated skill of thinking through diagrams, has limitless possibilities, but one diagram alone does have specific limitations. This leads us to consider possible pitfalls in the use of diagrams.

Some pitfalls

Almost anything can be achieved on paper, and in theory, so it can be quite difficult for some people to accept that diagrams do have practical application. The reaction to this problem is a temptation, for those who use diagrams, to make claims beyond what is possible. This is the *inappropriate-claim* pitfall. An Influence diagram or Mind Map is drawn and then the claim is made that the cause of the problem has been identified. Or, a Fishbone diagram is drawn and a claim made that the situation has been 'mapped'. Such examples of the inappropriate-claim pitfall should be avoided. Essentially, the drawing of diagrams can promise to enlighten our view of complex situations. If, as a result of this being achieved, a way is found to solve a difficult problem, the diagramming will have served a useful purpose. An error in this respect is to think that the act of diagramming will solve a problem. A spanner or a screwdriver cannot fix an engine, but the task is made so much easier when they are available. Diagrams are tools, and in the right hands can make the most complex situations understandable. To avoid this pitfall, be realistic about what each core diagram can do, whether to provide a broad overview, to identify causes and forces, or plan the way forward. When it is found that the use of one diagram has not fulfilled a need, do not hesitate to introduce another diagram that either complements the first or provides a more appropriate approach.

Diagrams use few words, so every word that is used must be chosen with great care. The *word-sloppiness* pitfall leads to a misuse of diagrams. Using a noun when a verb is essential can largely invalidate a diagram where the focus is on action. For anything to be the cause of something else there has got to be an action of some kind. Often diagrams are drawn in textbooks and papers supposedly showing cause and effect when inspection of the diagram shows that no such relationship could exist. At the root of this particular pitfall is a misunderstanding of causation; practice with Multiple-Cause diagrams should correct this misunderstanding where it exists. When a diagram represents a specific process, a few precise words are needed to capture the essence of what is being done. This practice is a good discipline because it helps people think more clearly and precisely about the process under consideration. To avoid this pitfall, inspect and 'weigh' each word that is used, just as you think about the most appropriate shapes and symbols when drawing a diagram.

There is a balance to be achieved between allowing your imagination full scope and maintaining some formal conventions for the purpose of communicating your ideas. The *over-elaboration* pitfall means being over-creative, when it is necessary to be clear and concise in what you have to say in diagram form. A fundamental aim in diagramming is simplicity – not always possible but an aim nevertheless. To avoid this pitfall, make use of the standard diagramming conventions that provide a framework; within this framework you can still exercise your imagination. There are no specific rules about how close to conventions you need to be, but the aim is to get the right balance between convention and creativeness. If you wish to ignore diagramming conventions altogether and be totally creative, those who 'read' your diagram will simply have to be of the same mind. When they are not of the same mind, you may have to explain your diagram at great length, which will tend to defeat its purpose.

A declared aim in diagramming is to 'keep it simple', but in doing this there is what can be called the *over-simplification* pitfall. Some people, seduced by the power of diagrams to clarify, can be tempted to build clarity and simplicity into the actual situation being diagrammed. Drawing a Multiple-Cause diagram of inner-city violence, or of serious political unrest between countries, could lead to this kind of pitfall. The diagramming of such situations is possible, but the generalized exploration diagrams (see Figure 11.1) represent possibly the limit of such diagramming. An overview provided in this way can be very enlightening, and can lead to more understanding of the situation, but it would be wrong to suggest that this will help to simplify the situation. Some problems cannot be solved, and in such cases a greater enlightenment helps us to cope more easily. The act of coping tends to be a much underrated behaviour. To avoid this pitfall, be clear in your own mind about the distinction between images on paper and reality on the ground. Be prepared to ask about any diagram, 'How close is it to reality?' If the answer is, 'Simply skimming the surface', then be ready to acknowledge this fact. Recognize that few diagrams can hope to cover all possible variables, whether dependent or independent, especially in very complex situations. The important thing is to know the limits of any one diagram in a particular context, and be prepared to use more than one type of diagram from your diagram toolbox. The subject of business management is littered with acronyms – TPM, RE, TQM, NLP, FMS, MRP, FMEA etc. – that often are solutions looking for problems. The use of diagrams should not fall into this trap. Apply diagrams only when needed; the 'toolbox of diagrams' metaphor should be kept in mind whenever diagrams are used.

12 A summary

Applying diagrams selectively

Fourteen core diagrams are covered in this book, but in presenting examples of how they can be used, fifty-nine diagrams have been drawn. An important skill is to recognize when a diagram will help, how to choose the kind of diagram that will offer most insight, and also, when presenting results to others, which diagram will have most impact. The basic rule is to ask yourself: 'What is my main concern here? Is it how things are controlled? Where does the main influence come from? What or who is actually involved? What change do we need to make?' Generally the act of drawing a diagram is made more effective when there is some focus like this. New ideas do emerge from diagramming, but they are ideas relevant to the problem rather than just any ideas. Playing around with diagrams can, in certain circumstances, be creative, but the most effective results seem to come from having direction in our diagramming work.

When drawing a diagram, it is more important to concentrate upon thinking rather than on how well the diagram is presented. The point that diagrams should be tools for thought is worth repeating. The roughest sketches can be as effective as anything from computer graphics, even though for publishing convenience these have been used in some chapters. Depending upon your style, the drawing on screen may be more conducive to thinking or you may find that a soft pencil is better. There are no strict rules about how diagrams are used. Where rules do exist, they cover the conventions for drawing specific diagrams. The reason we have these conventions is to provide a commonly recognized and shared means of communication. I am following similar conventions of sentence length, paragraphs and punctuation while typing this section; drawing diagrams is simply another form of communication.

Dealing with the conventions

Conventions in diagramming, as elsewhere, imply the use of rules;

however, rules are for the guidance of the wise, so depart from them if you know that an alternative diagram will communicate just as well, or even better, than the core diagrams given in this book. Diagramming offers scope for inventiveness and new, more imaginative images will go on being produced.

The diagram in Figure 11.3 departs from the 'core' approach, and is done for one person's benefit, yet the drawing ought to communicate something to others. Note what was said about reading diagrams in Chapter 3: beginning at the title, it is possible to see the subject of the diagram, and the nature of the links between events, in this case it is flow, but looking at the diagram you see that forces have also been included.

There is a reasonably clear start and possible finishing points rather than one exit. The work does begin with an idea, and this leads to some deliberation about how sound or unsound any book proposal would be. Family, friends and the diagram of SWOT are ideal for this purpose, and the essence of this exercise can be considered as drivers and restrainers in a Force-Field diagram.

The restrainers are seen as difficulties to be overcome rather than actual obstacles, but they do have to be addressed rather than relying upon the drivers alone to complete the task successfully.

The issue of some people not relating to diagrams was tackled by making this a subject early in the book. The appropriate focus continued to be an issue: instinctively my desire remained to have no real focus but to make diagramming more widely acceptable everywhere. People with a specialist business need would be discouraged by an approach that was too generalist, and those with a general interest in diagrams as a means of communicating or creativity would feel the same way about a business focus. Eventually a decision was made about an appropriate focus, but this does not mean that this particular restrainer has gone away. At some time it is likely that someone will produce a work on diagramming that has more general appeal. It was to avoid the charge of being too theoretical that I decided to include business-related sections and practical examples from different business activities, as well as the more general everyday examples.

Note the use of conventions in shapes: bubbles for 'soft', less certain activities, and boxes for 'hard' specific actions. The one diamond asks for a decision to be made, between proposing the book and going ahead and writing it; the latter decision was taken in this case. Unlike Flow-Process diagrams there are a number of different outcomes that are possible. For this reason, if one Flow-type diagram alone was chosen it would be an Algorithm which is most appropriate for showing alternative options. The working diagram has been shown in Figure 11.3 as a

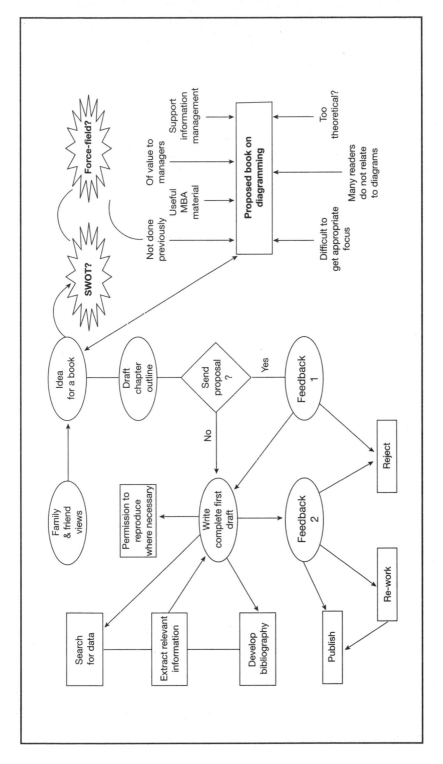

Figure 12.1 Composite diagram of writing this book

way of sharing with the reader a mix of diagram conventions and types that can be helpful to one person planning a book.

Finally thought needs to be given to choosing media for diagrams. There can be direct transfer of diagrams from computer screen to a large presentation, via an overhead projector, or direct projector. Film slides can be made and back-projected using more than one projector. People at remote locations can develop diagrams on a screen by using computer networking. Possibly the best medium, in a creative sense and for ready convenience, is still a large sheet of scrap paper. The cigarette packet type of canvas for drawing, mentioned at the beginning, is not so acceptable in these over-protective times, but still serves well as a message that diagrams can be drawn on virtually anything and any-where. Good diagramming!

Bibliography

Ahuja, H.N. et al. (1994) *Project Management Techniques in Planning and Control*. London: John Wiley.

Allwein, G. (ed.) (1996) *Logic Reasoning with Diagrams*. Oxford: Oxford University Press.

Annett, M. (1985) *Left, Right Hand and Brain: The Right Shift Theory*. London: Lawrence Erlbaum Associates.

Belbin, R.M. (1981) *Management Teams: Why They Succeed or Fail*. Oxford: Heinemann.

Belbin, R.M. (1993) *Roles at Work: A Strategy for Human Resource Management*. Oxford: Heinemann.

Budwar, P.S. (1996) *Cognitive Mapping Techniques to Study Managerial Conditions*. Manchester: Manchester Business School.

Burwell World Directory of Information Brokers (1997) Houston: Burwell Enterprises; London: TFPL.

Buzan, T. (1993) *The Mind Map Book*. London: BBC Books.

Craig, M. (1992) 'Techniques for analysis and techniques for investigation', in S. Truelove (ed.) *Handbook of Training and Development*. Oxford: Blackwell Business.

Dodgson, C.L. (Lewis Carroll) (1887) *The Game of Logic*. London.

Eden, C. and Radford, J. (1990) *Tackling Strategic Problems*. London: Sage.

Eden, C.L. et al. (1995) *Getting Started with Cognitive Mapping*. Glasgow: Banxia Software.

Edwards, B. (1982) *Drawing on the Right Side of the Brain*. London: Fontana Collins.

Feynman, R.P. (1985) *QED: The Strange Story of Light and Matter*. London: Penguin Books.

Gelb. M.J. (1995) *Thinking for a Change*. London: Aurum Press.

Howe, M.J.A. (1970) 'Repeated presentation and recall of meaningful prose'. *Journal of Educational Psychology*, **61**(3), 214–19.

Howe, M.J.A. (ed.) (1977) *Adult Learning*. London: John Wiley.

Huff, A.S. (ed.) (1990) *Mapping Strategic Thought*. New York: John Wiley.

Kelly, G.A. (1955) *The Psychology of Personal Constructs*, Vols 1 and 2. New York: Norton.

Lockyer, K. and Gordon, J. (1991) *Critical Path Analysis and Other Project Network Techniques*. London: Pitman Publishing.

Lowe, R. (1993) *Successful Instructional Diagrams*. London: Kogan Page.

McDermott, P. and Clarke, D.N. (1998) *Mind Maps in Medicine*. London: Harcourt Brace.

Marrow, A.J. (1969) *Kurt Lewin, the Practising Theorist*. New York.

Maruyama, M. (1963) 'The second cybernetics: deviation, amplifying mutual causal processes'. *The American Scientist*, **51**(2).

Masters, A. (1980) *Mind Map*. (Palmistry) London: Eyre Methuen.

Moder, J.J. et al. (1983) *Project Management with CPM, PERT and Precedence Diagramming*. London: Van Nostrand Reinhold.

Pask, G. and Scott, B.C.E (1972) 'Learning strategies and individual competence'. *International Journal of Man Machine Studies*, **4**(3), 217–53.

Regnard, C. (1995) *Flow Diagrams in Advanced Cancer and Other Diseases*. London: Edward Arnold.

Rosenau, M.D. (1992) *Successful Project Management: A Step by Step Approach*. New York: Van Nostrand Reinhold.

Rouse, W.B. (1998) 'Knowledge maps for knowledge mining: Application to R&D Technology Management'. *IEEE Transactions on Systems, Man and Cybernetics*, **28**(3).

Shin, S.J. (1994) *The Logic Status of Diagrams*. Cambridge: Cambridge University Press.

Tustin, E. (1953) *The Mechanism of Economic Systems*. Cambridge, Mass: Harvard University Press.

Van Gundy, A.B. (1998) *The Techniques of Structured Problem Solving*. New York: Van Nostrand Reinhold.

Warnken, K. (1981) *The Information Brokers*. New York: R.R. Bowker.

Appendix A
Matrix of core diagrams to themes

Core diagrams	Mapping business	Influence/ relation- ship	Causa- tion	Control	Change	Flow	Handling informa- tion
Algorithm				•		••	•
Control		•		••	•	•	•
Fishbone		•	••		•		•
Flow		•		•		••	
Force- field		•	••		••		
Influence	••	••		•	••		•
Input- output				••	••	••	•
Map	••				••		••
Multiple- cause		••	••		••		
Relation- ship		••			•	•	•
Ring		••			••	••	
Sign		••	••		••	•	•
Tree	••	••	•		•	••	••
Window	•	••	•		••		••

Code: • = applicable •• = highly applicable

Appendix B
Matrix of core diagrams to management activity

Core diagrams	Problem solving	Decision making	Organization structure	Group working	Project management	Writing reports	Preparing presentation
Algorithm	•	••		•	••	•	•
Control	•	•		•	••	•	
Fishbone	••	•		•	••	•	
Flow	•	••		•	••	••	••
Force-field	••	••		••	••	•	
Influence	•	•	••	••	•	••	••
Input-output	•	•			••		•
Map		•	••	•	•	••	••
Multiple-cause	••	••		••	••	•	•
Relationship	•		••	••	•	••	••
Ring	•	•	•		••		•
Sign	••	••		••	••	•	
Tree	•	••	••	•	••	•	
Window	•	•		••	••		

Code: • = applicable   •• = highly applicable

Index